**REPORT OF THE
SELECT COMMITTEE
ON
MANPOWER TRAINING**

Ontario Legislative Assembly

REPORT OF THE SELECT COMMITTEE
ON
MANPOWER TRAINING

Hon. J. R. Simonett, Chairman / February, 1963

THE SELECT COMMITTEE ON MANPOWER TRAINING

ON APRIL 18, 1962, the following resolution was adopted by the Legislative Assembly:

> "That a Select Committee of the House be appointed to examine, investigate, inquire into, study and make recommendations concerning:
>
> 1. The Apprenticeship Act and the regulations made thereunder;
>
> 2. All aspects of the apprenticeship system as presently established in Ontario and more particularly as it pertains to the training of persons in trades or crafts relating to the construction industry and in industrial undertakings;
>
> 3. The training of workers and more particularly retraining and upgrading of skills; and
>
> 4. The roles of government, industry and labour in this field."

It was further provided that the Committee would consist of eleven members, as follows:

Hon. J. R. Simonett, M.P.P., Chairman
Mr. R. J. Boyer, M.P.P.
Mr. Rene Brunelle, M.P.P.
Mr. Alex Carruthers, M.P.P.
Mr. John Chapple, M.P.P.
Mr. R. W. Gisborn, M.P.P.
Mr. R. J. Harris, M.P.P.
Mr. Jules Morin, M.P.P.
Mr. Ellis P. Morningstar, M.P.P.
Mr. Andrew E. Thompson, M.P.P.
Mr. John H. White, M.P.P.

Dr. John H. G. Crispo, Assistant Professor of Industrial Relations, School of Business, University of Toronto, was responsible for the drafting of the Report and served as the Committee's Director of Research. Mr. T. M. Eberlee, Assistant Deputy Minister of Labour, acted as the Committee's Secretary.

The Committee commenced its work in May, 1962, with background studies of a wide range of matters relating to its terms of reference. During the summer, it invited representations from interested parties and in the fall and winter received, studied and held public hearings on briefs and submissions from a number of individuals and organizations. A list of those who submitted presentations is contained in the Appendix of the Report.

The Committee is grateful to all who contributed to the clarification of the many complex issues which faced it. In addition to those who submitted briefs, it wishes to make particular record of its thanks to Professor Harold A. Logan; Dr. S. D. Rendall, Superintendent of Secondary Education, Department of Education; Mr. L. M. Johnston, Assistant Superintendent of Secondary Education; Mr. D. C. McNeill, Director of Apprenticeship, Department of Labour; Mrs. Josephine Grimshaw, Economist, Department of Labour; Mr. C. R. Ford, Director of the Technical and Vocational Training Branch, Federal Department of Labour; Dr. Gil Schonning, Assistant Director, Economics and Statistics Branch, Federal Department of Labour; Dr. Seymour Wolfbein, and the members of the staff of the Office of Manpower, Automation and Training, United States Department of Labour, and Mr. Arnold Weinrib, a member of the Committee's staff. The Committee also desires to express appreciation for the co-operation and advice of Labour and Education Department officials in the other provinces of Canada. To the many others who extended assistance to the Committee and its staff, we express our gratitude.

Studies and other background material including the transcript of the Committee's hearings and discussions, will be placed on file in the Library of the Legislative Assembly for reference by all who may be interested in further, detailed investigation in this field.

· · · · · ·

The Committee believes that its work can now be ended and begs to submit the following report which represents the unanimous conclusions of its members on the matters referred to it.

TABLE OF CONTENTS

	Page
INTRODUCTION	1
The Committee's Terms of Reference	1
The Plan of the Report	2
PART I—THE PROBLEM, BASIC PREMISES AND GENERAL OBJECTIVES	5
Recent Developments in the Canadian Labour Force:	
A Statement of the Problem	5
Factors Affecting the Occupational Composition of the Labour Force	5
An Accelerating Rate of Change	7
Trends in the Occupational Composition of the Labour Force	8
The Present Quality of the Canadian Labour Force	10
The Relationship Between Education and Training and Unemployment—A Word of Caution	14
Basic Premises—The Assumptions which Underlie This Report	16
General Objectives	17
PART II—A BRIEF REVIEW OF ONTARIO'S PRESENT VOCATIONAL EDUCATION AND TRAINING SYSTEM	25
PART III—COMMENTS AND RECOMMENDATIONS WITH REGARD TO SPECIFIC FACETS OF OUR EXISTING EDUCATIONAL AND TRAINING SYSTEM	29
The Robarts Plan—Some Additional Observations	29
An Expanding Role for the Trade Schools	33
Our Growing Need for Technicians—The Role of the Technical Institutes	34
The University Crisis	36

	Page
Apprenticeship in the Building Trades	37
Apprenticeship in Other Trades and Occupations Outside of General Industry	49
Apprenticeship in General Industry—The Need for a Separate and Distinct Approach	50
Other Forms of Training in General Industry	53
Special Programs for Training or Retraining Particular Categories of Adult Workers	54
Salvaging Dropouts and Enhancing Their Employability	54
Training Unemployed Workers Who Have Obsolete Skills or Who are Relatively Unskilled	56
Upgrading of Employed Persons Who Otherwise would be Displaced from their Jobs	60
Facilitating the Integration of Immigrants into Constructive Employment	61
Rehabilitating Inmates of Penal Institutions	65
Rehabilitating Disabled and Handicapped Persons	66
The Role of Private Trade Schools and Correspondence Schools	68
Supervisory Training and Management Development	69

PART IV—RELATED COMMENTS AND RECOMMENDATIONS — 71

Research—A Neglected but Vital Need	71
Forecasting Changes in the Nature and Composition of the Labour Force	71
Developing and Improving our Educational and Training Methods	76
Assessing the Record	76
Responsibility for Research	77
Vocational Guidance	78
Establishing Common Standards and Facilitating Upward Movement Within the Occupational Hierarchy	81
The Need for Common Standards Applicable to the Various Levels Within the Occupational Hierarchy	82
Facilitating Upward Movement Within the Occupational Hierarchy	86

	Page
Providing Adequate Numbers of Vocational Teachers	88
Planning—The Need for a Provincial Advisory Council on Vocational and Industrial Education	89
The Administration of Vocational and Industrial Education in Ontario	91

PART V—JUSTIFYING THE COSTS AND SHARING THE RESPONSIBILITIES FOR A COMPREHENSIVE EDUCATIONAL AND TRAINING SYSTEM — 95

Justifying the Costs of a Comprehensive Educational and Training System	95
Sharing the Responsibilities for a Comprehensive Educational and Training System	100

SUMMARY AND CONCLUSIONS	105
General Objectives	105
Specific Recommendations	106
APPENDIX	125

INTRODUCTION

THE COMMITTEE'S TERMS OF REFERENCE

THIS COMMITTEE was assigned the task of outlining what is required in this Province to provide the people of Ontario with a comprehensive and up-to-date vocational education and training system. We undertook an investigation of virtually the entire range of manpower training and development programs in Ontario: full-time courses in secondary schools, trade schools, and technical institutes as well as part-time extension programs therein; training for employable unemployed as well as measures designed to upgrade those already employed; and formal apprenticeship programs as well as less formalized methods for occupational betterment and advancement.

To make our task more manageable, however, the Committee decided to accept the Robarts Plan as an appropriate construct at the secondary school level and to concentrate on our needs, exclusive of the universities, beyond that level. Thus, aside from a limited number of recommendations pertaining to the Robarts Plan and the universities, the Committee has devoted the bulk of its attention to other phases of our vocational education and training system.

The Committee has not concerned itself with the academic side of our educational and training system. This does not reflect any minimization of the importance of producing the "whole man." Indeed, as the time we are able to devote to leisure activities increases, this objective is likely to become ever more significant. At the same time, however, because the task of developing the "employable man" is becoming increasingly complex, more and more of our time and effort will be demanded for this purpose.

Although many of the attributes of the whole man can be imparted to the student or worker at the same time he receives his vocational preparation, the time which can be devoted to such matters will leave much to be desired. For this reason we welcome the tremendous variety of academic and cultural enrichment courses which are being offered in night classes in many centres across this Province. For those who have developed a marketable skill, these courses afford an excellent opportunity to pursue their non-vocational interests.

Reverting to the distinction which has been drawn between the whole man and the employable man, it does seem reasonable to assert that unless we turn out employable men we cannot hope to develop whole men. This is not to imply that the man who is well trained academically is likely to find himself without a job. For a growing number of occupations especially in the white collar field—this is anything but the case. Nonetheless, while a sound academic background is always advantageous, it does remain true that for the majority of potential job-holders something beyond a straight academic education remains a necessity. Historically, we in Ontario have tended to emphasize academic preparation, often at the expense of vocational education and training.[1] It is vital that this imbalance be corrected as quickly as possible.

THE PLAN OF THE REPORT

This Report is divided into five major parts. In the first Part we begin by analysing the nature of the challenge which confronts us in the field of manpower training and development. We then set forth the assumptions upon which we have based our findings and outline the general guide-lines or objectives which we feel should underlie all of our efforts in the field of vocational education and training.

Part II of the Report describes Ontario's present educational and training system and sets the stage for the more detailed parts which follow.

Parts III and IV of the Report move from the general to the particular. In Part III we make a number of comments and recommendations on specific facets of our existing educational and training

---

[1] Prior to the expansion which began in 1960, the last technical high school which was built in this Province was completed in 1953. Also of significance is the fact that only one trade school was in operation in Ontario until last year.

system. This is followed, in Part IV, by an equally specific treatment of a number of related matters. Such things as the need for common standards and continued research and the administration of vocational and industrial education in this Province are dealt with in some detail. Understandably, these are the longest and most comprehensive parts of the Report.

Part V of the Report is devoted to two questions. The first relates to the matter of justifying the costs of a comprehensive educational and training system and the second pertains to the respective responsibilities of different groups in society for the provision of such a system.

PART I

THE PROBLEM, BASIC PREMISES AND GENERAL OBJECTIVES

RECENT DEVELOPMENTS IN THE CANADIAN LABOUR FORCE
A STATEMENT OF THE PROBLEM

THE occupational composition of the Canadian labour force has been undergoing pronounced changes for a number of decades. Since the war there appears to have been an acceleration in the rate of these changes.

Factors Affecting the Occupational Composition of the Labour Force

Among the more important developments accounting for recent changes in the labour force in Canada are the following:

(1) TECHNOLOGICAL CHANGE

The importance of technological change is not to be minimized. Regardless of the form taken by such changes—whether they entail a modification in the nature of the good or service which is being produced or a change in materials or techniques—there is bound to be an effect on the way in which the various factors of production are combined. Almost invariably this will involve a change in total manpower requirements and/or a change in the composition of those requirements.

(2) RESEARCH AND DEVELOPMENT

Associated with the effects of technological changes themselves are the increased expenditures required to ensure further technological progress. Additional outlays for research and development are bound to increase our high-level manpower requirements. It should be noted, however, that because we import so much of the technology which is applied in this country, our manpower needs for research and development are likely to remain somewhat lower than otherwise would be the case.

(3) DEFENSE AND FOREIGN AID COMMITMENTS

Just as important as the impact of research and development on our manpower needs is the potential effect of defense and foreign aid commitments. With the technology of warfare now so advanced and with increasing emphasis being given to technical assistance in the field of foreign aid, it is obvious that any change in the level of our activities in either of these spheres could have significant consequences in terms of our overall manpower requirements.

(4) INSTITUTIONAL POLICIES AND PRACTICES

Although it is difficult to find specific evidence on this point, the Committee suspects that such things as new techniques in personnel management may also have a significant bearing on our manpower requirements. Emphasis on a policy of promotion from within, for example, can lead to higher hiring standards at a firm's lower intake levels than would otherwise be the case. Contrariwise, the use of "scientific management" to break down tasks into the simplest possible components could readily reduce the quality of labour required by a firm.

(5) CHANGES IN THE COMPOSITION OF CONSUMER DEMAND

Perhaps more important than any other factor in the long run are the changes which take place in the public's buying habits and requirements. Historically, as the demands made upon the Canadian economy diversified, and secondary industries grew relative to primary activities, the composition of the labour force also changed. Likewise, it is probable that the on-going shift in favour of the service sectors of the economy will continue to have a marked effect on our labour requirements.

(6) FOREIGN TRADE DEVELOPMENTS

Added to the above considerations are the potential effects which international trade re-alignments could have on the Canadian labour force. If Canada is caught up in the general movement for freer trade which is now sweeping the western world, the nature of our economy could be radically affected. Although this would soon show up in the form of a change in the relative significance of our primary, secondary and tertiary activities, and thus would be reflected in changes in the composition of demand, it is a factor of sufficient importance to warrant separate attention.

(7) REGIONAL SHIFTS IN THE DISTRIBUTION OF INDUSTRY

Of particular concern to Ontario is the role which this Province is likely to play in the continuing development of Canada. Should there be any change in the distribution of economic activities between the various provinces, this could have a significant effect on manpower requirements in Ontario. Although there has been no evidence of any such shift in the recent past, it is well to realize that there are regional variables as well as national considerations to be borne in mind.

An Accelerating Rate of Change

Just as important as the factors listed above are the rates at which changes in these factors take place. In recent years there is a good deal of evidence to suggest that these changes have been taking place at an accelerating rate. Large expenditures on research and development, for example, are a relatively new phenomenon. Moreover, we have also gained the impression that changes in the composition of demand may be occurring at a more rapid rate than in the past.

More pronounced than either of these developments, however, is the fact that the pace of technological change may be quickening. In very large measure this is no doubt due to the "industry of discovery" which has been created in order to stimulate such change. This has not only led to expanded work in the field of pure research but has significantly reduced the time which it takes to apply the results of such research. This point was stressed in a recent speech by a high official of the Federal Department of Labour:

> The gap between scientific discovery and industrial application has been rapidly shrinking. Michael Faraday's discovery of electricity was not applied for fifty years. The average gap today between discovery and application is only five to eight years.[1]

That this matter has caused concern outside of government circles is apparent from the attention given to it in a recent booklet published by the Canadian Association for Adult Education:

> Recent changes have been more frequent, drastic and complex, and consequently manpower requirements are changing more drastically and rapidly than during any previous period.[2]

The point is that the factors which affect the overall level and the skill composition of our labour requirements seem to be changing more rapidly than in the past. This has prompted one official of the Department of Labour in Ottawa to venture the following prediction:

> It is expected that the great occupational shifts within the Canadian labour force are likely to continue at an even more rapid pace in the decade ahead (than they did in the nineteen-fifties).[3]

If this is a valid conclusion, it means that it will become increasingly difficult to predict and prepare in advance for future labour force developments. It will also tend to mean that fewer and fewer workers will be able to follow one trade or occupation for their lifetimes.

Trends in the Occupational Composition of the Labour Force

The forces already described have so affected the occupational composition of our labour force as to induce a general and even sharp upturn in the level of our skill requirements. This is clear from a

---
[1] W. R. Dymond, Assistant Deputy Minister, Department of Labour, Ottawa, "Manpower Implications of Technological Change", (A Paper delivered to the Ontario Chapter of the International Association of Personnel in Employment Security, Toronto, September 14, 1962) p. 1.
[2] Fred E. Whitworth, Co-Ordinator of Special Projects and Secretary of the Vocational-Technical Education Project, Canadian Conference on Education, *Skills for Tomorrow*, (Canadian Conference on Education, Published under a Grant from the Ford Foundation, 1962) p. 22.
[3] C. R. Ford, "The Federal Government Looks at Technical Education", (A Paper delivered to the Ontario Headmasters Association, Kingston, August 17, 1961) p. 5.

review of labour force developments between 1949 and 1959. Especially revealing are figures presented to the Special Committee of the Senate on Manpower and Employment by the Canadian Welfare Council.[1] They showed that while the total Canadian labour force in Canada grew by approximately 24% between 1949 and 1959, occupations which are skilled or relatively skilled grew much faster:

—Professional workers increased by 71%
—Skilled occupations increased by 38%
—White collar jobs in general increased by 34%

As is readily apparent, the more highly qualified among this group of relatively skilled occupations grew even faster than their less demanding counterparts.

At the opposite end of the skill spectrum equally significant developments took place. Jobs open to unskilled or semi-skilled workers increased by 19%, considerably less than the overall increase in the labour force as a whole. At the same time, opportunities in our primary industries—a high proportion of which are unskilled or semi-skilled—decreased by 27%.

Similar trends in almost all industrialized countries attest to the general validity of these figures. Moreover, detailed studies of a number of firms in a variety of manufacturing industries in this country have revealed parallel, although less extreme, developments. These findings have been summarized as follows:

> The rapid shift in the occupational composition of these industries towards non-clerical, white-collar occupations and in the plant to the maintenance trades and some production tradesmen is clearly evident. These shifts are further evidence of the growing emphasis on manpower requirements with relatively high degrees of skill, technical knowledge and specialist training of a variety of kinds.[2]

Reflecting the general and persistent tendency for the overall level of our skill requirements to rise, it has recently been estimated that jobs which can be filled by employees with little or no skill account

---

[1] Canadian Welfare Council, "Submission to Special Committee on Manpower and Employment," in the Senate of Canada, *Proceedings of the Special Committee of the Senate on Manpower and Employment* (Queen's Printer, Ottawa, 1961) p. 1256. These figures were based on data prepared for the Royal Commission on Canada's Economic Prospects in 1957.

[2] W. R. Dymond, "Manpower Implications of Technological Change", op. cit., p. 8.

for only about 30% of employment.[1] There is every reason to believe —based at least on our experience over the past few years—that this proportion will continue to diminish in size. How small it may eventually become is difficult to say. Should the present trend persist indefinitely a social problem of major proportions could easily result.

Whether we care to admit it or not there will probably always be a significant minority of our work force which will not be able to do anything but relatively unskilled work. Although there is little evidence to date to suggest that we are reaching the point where we will have fewer unskilled jobs available than workers who are capable of nothing more demanding, such a possibility is not as remote as it once was. Nonetheless, it would be most misleading to suggest that we are even approaching that point at the present time. While we have had more unskilled workers than unskilled jobs in recent years, we have only begun to do something about upgrading the skills of the former. Only when we have exhausted our efforts in this regard and are unable to find sufficient jobs for those incapable of rising above the unskilled level, will we be in serious difficulty. It is to be emphasized, however, that we are far from being as knowledgeable in this area as we should be.

Just as important as the rising level of our general skill requirements are the changes which can be expected to take place in the types of skills demanded. There will probably be an increasing need for workers with greater conceptual ability, for workers who can think through and resolve complicated problems, for workers who can analyze and synthesize. The challenge of developing this type of worker will no doubt prove more demanding than the relatively simple task of upgrading workers in the more traditional skills.

The Present Quality of the Canadian Labour Force

In the face of the trends now apparent on the demand side of the labour market, it is disturbing to realize how inadequate the situation is on the supply side of the market. It is not our purpose to attempt to assess the general quality of the labour force in Ontario, let alone in Canada. Such an undertaking is beyond our resources. Instead we

---

[1]Information Branch, Department of Labour, Ottawa, *Education, Training, and Employment* (Queen's Printer, Ottawa, 1961) p. 9.

have focused on the situation among those readily available for employment. This includes both unemployed persons and those who are currently leaving the school system. With neither group is there any ground for complacency.

The situation among the unemployed is particularly disturbing. A survey conducted by the National Employment Service in 1955 showed that 70.2% of persons seeking work through N.E.S. offices had an educational level of Grade VIII or less. Although data prepared for the Special Committee of the Senate on Manpower and Employment revealed considerable improvement in the situation by 1960, even then 55% of those registered with the N.E.S. had no more than a Grade VIII education. The desperate plight of such individuals is reflected in the varying incidence of unemployment among those with different amounts of education. Recent surveys have revealed that there is a clear relationship between lack of education and unemployment. In one study, for example, it was shown that the impact of unemployment was over six times heavier among those who did not complete primary school than among those who had completed secondary school.[1]

In their present state, it is clear, most of our unemployed workers are in no position to compete effectively in the present-day world of work. If the occupational shifts discussed earlier in this Report continue, their position will become more and more disadvantageous with every passing year.

In the long run, the only way to overcome this situation is to provide workers with more education and training before they actually enter the labour force. Judging by the current rate of our "drop-outs," we still have a long way to go in this regard. A special study prepared by the Dominion Bureau of Statistics[2] in 1960 showed that only 66% of those beginning Grade II after the War were likely to enter first year of secondary school. Only half of the 66% would survive to enter the year of junior leaving (Grade XII in Ontario, New Brunswick and British Columbia and Grade XI elsewhere) and less than half of these would ever attend the final year of secondary school. Taking into account the extra year of high school offered in this

[1] The Senate of Canada, *The Report of the Special Committee of the Senate on Manpower and Employment*, (Queen's Printer, Ottawa, 1961) Table 28, p. 61.
[2] Dominion Bureau of Statistics, *Student Progress Through the Schools*, (Queen's Printer, Ottawa, 1960).

Province (as well as in New Brunswick and British Columbia), Ontario compared quite favourably with the other jurisdictions. 34% of our Grade II students entered Grade XII and 15% entered Grade XIII.

Since this survey was conducted the record in the Province has improved steadily. In their appearance before the Committee, for example, Department of Education personnel revealed that over 40% of those who entered Grade II in the early fifties are now successfully completing Grade XII and that a growing proportion of these are entering and graduating from Grade XIII. Looking at it from another point of view, the improvement has been even more impressive. Whereas in the academic year 1946-1947, only 36% of those between the ages of 15 and 19 were in school in Ontario, the corresponding figure was 65% in 1961-1962.

Much of this improvement has been due to the efforts of educationists and of others interested in young people. A good deal of it, however, has no doubt been due to other factors. It must be remembered, for example, that the labour market has been so depressed in recent years, especially for unskilled young people, that there has been a strong incentive to remain in school. This would probably have led to higher retention rates even if there had been no advancements in the field of education. In fact, of course, there were a number of significant developments during the period under review. The district high school program by itself has had a tremendous impact. So have the individual efforts of a number of outstanding municipal school boards.

The point is that as effective as these changes within the school system may have been in retaining more of our youths in school for longer periods of time, they have been strongly reinforced by external considerations. Despite the latter our record of progress to date still leaves much to be desired. We must continue to make progress in this area if we are to equip the workers of the future with sufficient education and training to fill the types of job openings likely to be available to them.

Not only must we provide students with sufficient education and training but we must also make sure that it is of the right kind. There is a qualitative as well as a quantitative problem. More education and training by itself will solve nothing. Unless it is appropriate to the types of work our students are going to find available for them it will not serve the intended purpose. In the past, unfortunately, this has not always been the case. Thus, in addition to the drop-out problem we have often found ourselves turning out students who were not functionally prepared for the type of work they ended up doing.

Unless we provide appropriate amounts and kinds of education and training we cannot hope to furnish the members of our work force with any degree of long term employment security. To fail in this regard will not only be disastrous for the individuals involved but will also jeopardize the future growth and prosperity of this Province. Because immigration can no longer be counted on to supply us with the steady flow of skilled talent we require, we must either develop these talents internally or suffer serious skill shortages which are bound to slow down our rate of economic growth. Even if we could continue to rely on immigration to fill such shortages, it is questionable whether we should resort to such an expedient. It does not seem fair to rely on immigration and fail to give native-born Canadians a chance to prepare themselves for our high-level manpower requirements.

For many years after World War II we were able to fill many of our high level manpower requirements by means of immigration. In many of the skilled trades, for example, Federal Department of Labour studies have shown that we were long able to count on immigration for one third or more of our needs. Because of the ready availability of such talent we were able to place less emphasis on our education and training facilities than was desirable from a long-range point of view. In the meantime, however, as employment at unheralded wages returned to most West European countries Canada began to experience serious unemployment. To the skilled worker in Europe emigration to Canada thus became less appealing. In more recent years, therefore, Canada has been forced to fall back on its own resources. This experience has made us more fully aware of existing deficiencies in our education and training system.

Although a large proportion of the foreign influx into the Canadian labour force since the war has been of a highly skilled order, many immigrants—especially in recent years—have arrived here with little education and training. Their deficiencies are similar to those of the native-born Canadian who drops out of school at an early age but they are often compounded by a lack of fluency in the English language. They thus present a somewhat specialized example of the overall problem we face in this area.

The Relationship Between Education and Training and Unemployment—A Word of Caution

In the face of the foregoing evidence, it may seem logical to argue that education and training can provide the key to full employment. As the incidence of unemployment has consistently been much greater among the less educated, and in the face of continuing shortages in a number of skilled trades and occupations, it is only natural that this view should gain some credence. It has become all too fashionable to claim that people are unemployed simply because they do not have appropriate training or skills and that the way to solve the problem of unemployment is to provide suitable upgrading and training programs.

Close analysis of this proposition reveals that it is not sound. Full employment depends much more upon an adequate level of aggregate demand than it does upon the skills of a country's labour force. General unemployment is thus more likely to be eradicated by appropriate fiscal and monetary policies than it is by large expenditures on education and training.

At the same time, however, the role which education and training can play in alleviating unemployment should not be minimized. While a general upgrading of the labour force cannot be counted on to eliminate the excess unemployment experienced in recent years, it can be expected to facilitate its reduction. At the very least a better trained work force would help us to maintain or possibly better our position in the world markets in which we must compete. Moreover, to the extent that further education and training contributed to more versatility within the labour force, it could contribute to a lessening of certain types of unemployment. (Such as those caused by frictional and/or structural considerations). In these and other respects there is probably a higher correlation than is generally appreciated between the relative skill of a country's labour force and the ease with which it may be kept fully employed.

This has been illustrated by recent experience in both Canada and the United States. At the same time that we have been experiencing a considerable amount of general unemployment, we have found ourselves confronted with shortages in a number of skilled occupations. A perusal of the records of the National Employment Service reveals that even during the most serious periods of unemployment in recent years, there have been insufficient qualified applicants available for a variety of skilled occupations. This suggests that if our labour force had been better prepared to meet the shifts which have been taking place in the level of our skill requirements, it would have certainly reduced the level of general unemployment in Canada.

Here again, however, the qualitative problem arises. The significance of the contribution which education and training can make to the reduction of unemployment will depend very much on the suitability of the education and training which is offered. If our efforts in this area are channeled in the wrong direction we could end up with nothing more than unemployed skilled workers instead of unemployed unskilled ones.

For a single province such as Ontario, there is a further point to be considered. While education and training do not have an overriding effect upon the general level of employment, degrees of skill attainment do appear to determine who is and who is not employed. To the extent that this is true, it follows that Ontario may be able to reduce its share of unemployment in Canada by maintaining a relatively highly qualified labour force.

Beyond the question of general unemployment there are the particular problems which are associated with certain categories of the unemployed. While upgrading and retraining may help the unemployed adult to find a job, he may be faced with other difficulties as well. For the unskilled older man, for example, there are likely to be other obstacles to employment besides a lack of education and training. Unless something is done to overcome age barriers, upgrading and retraining measures may not be as effective as they should be.

The point is that while education and training can make a contribution to the reduction of unemployment, we must not allow ourselves to be deluded into believing that by themselves they will serve this purpose. Neglect of traditional anti-cyclical weapons and special programs geared to the needs of particular groups, in the hope that vast expenditures on education and training might provide the key to full employment, would be a major mistake.

BASIC PREMISES—THE ASSUMPTIONS WHICH UNDERLIE THIS REPORT

In approaching the task before it, the Committee found it useful to delineate a number of assumptions. To appreciate the overall objectives set forth in the next section and the more specific recommendations which follow, these assumptions must be made clear.

(1) In the first place we have made the broad assumption that no radical rupture is likely to occur in the social, political or economic structure of the Province within the forseeable future.

(2) We are also postulating that there will be no fundamental change in the present distribution of responsibilities — financial or otherwise — between the various levels of government which are involved in the provision of education and training in this Province. (In this connection it is to be noted that special committees have recently been appointed by both the Ontario and Federal Governments to review the existing distribution of financial responsibilities between the various levels of government—municipal, provincial and federal—in this country. As these committees will almost certainly deal with the question of education and training costs, it would serve no real purpose for this Committee to involve itself in any detailed fashion in these matters. We will thus confine ourselves to a limited number of broad generalizations.)

(3) In the years ahead, we can expect our labour requirements to undergo constant and perhaps even an accelerating rate of change. This means that the initial acquistion of a particular trade or skill may not be enough to provide a worker with a means of livelihood for a prolonged period of time.

Federal Department of Labour officials have emphasized this point on a number of occasions. Typical of their many pronouncements is the following:

> The implications of our research are that the average worker in the labour force cannot expect to remain continually for 40 or 50 years in a single occupation with a given set of unchanging skills. He will constantly have to adjust to new employment demands and on occasion even make shifts to completely new occupations at higher levels of skill.[1]

---
[1] W. R. Dymond, "Manpower Implications of Technological Change", op. cit. p. 13.

(4) At this point in time it also seems reasonably safe to assert that there will be a persistent and continuing tendency for the general level of our skill requirements to rise. As a consequence, jobs available for well educated and highly trained workers will become relatively more numerous while occupations requiring semi-skilled or unskilled workers will become relatively fewer.

(5) For convenience we have also assumed that we will be sufficiently adept in manipulating our economic destiny to maintain a reasonably high level of employment. We make this assumption in order to be free to concentrate on our general needs in the field of education and training, exclusive of the supplementary role which education and training should be expected to play in our overall effort to reduce the level of unemployment.

(6) As well as assuming that full employment is a desirable goal (as we have done by implication, if nothing more, in the previous section), we have also assumed that we must strive for as skilled and productive a work force as is necessary to keep up with nations with which we must compete. This is essential if this country is to maintain itself as a viable economic entity and is to grow and prosper at a satisfactory rate. We have presumed that these are underlying objectives with which few will have any quarrel.

(7) As Canada's most diversified and highly-industrialized Province, we feel that Ontario has both a need and an obligation to be in the forefront in the field of manpower training and development. We have therefore proceeded on the assumption that our findings could have a profound influence upon other provinces which might choose to emulate some of the changes which are introduced as a result of this Report. This has led this Committee to approach its task in an even more serious frame of mind than might otherwise have been the case.

GENERAL OBJECTIVES

Having outlined our assumptions, we now turn to the general objectives which we feel should underlie the overall approach to manpower training and development in this Province. These broad objectives will set the stage for the many recommendations which are put forward in later sections of the Report.

(1) We must strive to increase the "holding-power" of our schools as much as possible. This is vital if we are to begin to provide the bulk of the new entrants into the labour force with any appreciable degree of long-run employment security. By cutting down on the number of drop-outs we would also reduce the most serious problems presently associated with the training of the unemployed. Because so many of those who have recently been exposed to unemployment lack a basic education, we are compelled to attempt to upgrade them academically either before or at the same time we try to train them.

In the present context, the term drop-out is applied only to those students who leave school without executing a complete educational plan. This does not mean that everyone should be expected to complete Grade XIII. For many students more limited attainments must be expected. The point is that drop-out should be defined in relation to varying standards. Only when the student fails to complete a designated program should he be classified as a drop-out.

Ideally, of course, the program which each student is expected to complete should be tailored to his particular capacity. Although such an ideal may be beyond practicality, every step which we take in this direction will contribute to the reduction of the drop-out problem. The point is that the best way to increase the holding power of our schools is to offer a sufficient variety of courses to appeal to the differing interests, abilities and aptitudes of our student population.

(2) In order to prepare workers for the periodic retraining they may have to undergo in the future, more emphasis will have to be placed on ability to learn and ability to adapt, as opposed simply to the acquistion of a limited range of manipulative skills. With regard to the formal school system, this will require that we keep our educational programs—especially on the vocational side—as broadly based as possible. By this we mean that the emphasis should not be placed on the acquisition of particular specialized skills during the first few years of vocational education. Instead two things should be emphasized. In so far as shopwork is concerned attention should be focused on training in families of related occupations. Initially, for example, training should be given in the automotive trades as a whole rather than in any one branch of those trades.

As regards directly related classroom instruction, it is becoming increasingly apparent that more and more time will have to be devoted to the academic fundamentals (such as mathematics and science in the technical fields and English in the clerical field) which are becoming ever more essential to a solid foundation in many occupations. This will not only serve to better prepare students for work but will also make it easier for vocational students to go on to some form of advanced post-high school training should they eventually decide to do so.

By concentrating on broad vocational preparation during the initial period of vocational training, we will enable students to develop a sufficient breadth of knowledge to readily adapt to the adjustments which are likely to be required of them in the future. The need for greater adaptability on the part of employees was strongly emphasized by the Ontario Division of the Canadian Manufacturers' Association in its submission to this Committee (Proceedings, pp. 1524-25):

> The most pressing need is for employees who, though lacking a specified skill, are capable of being re-trained or up-graded as the need arises or is foreseen. The worker lacking basic academic education becomes largely unemployable when his job ceases to exist in its present form due to technological or market changes. Thus "basic training for skill development" is the essential for all workers. This means a good basic knowledge in, for example, elementary mathematics, the ability to communicate clearly in English, elementary science and, most important of all, the ability to absorb further training.

Reflecting a similar point of view, the Ontario Industrial Education Council offered the following advice with respect to our secondary school programs (Proceedings, pp. 614-5):

> (The secondary schools should concentrate on training) in which the primary emphasis is on the development of the individual in relation to his capacity in theoretical knowledge and some illustrative applications and development in the ability to reason and analyse and synthesize.
>
> This is emphasized here in order to point up the danger there can be in confining to particular manipulative skills and practices. There may well have been too much attention to seeking to train for "a job" rather than laying a foundation in knowledge, reasoning ability and work organization that is going to be an asset through the individual's career. Secondary schools should be concerned with laying the foundation for the later specialization; they should not be confining the individual by attempting to deal with the "specialization" itself and which is going to be quickly outdated.

Since adaptability is in part a function of intelligence, we cannot expect all of our students to respond to this type of approach. For those who cannot absorb this type of knowledge, specialized vocational training in the less demanding trades and occupations is the only answer.

For the bulk of our student population, however, this should not prove to be an insurmountable obstacle. As long as the "foundation" content of the various courses is tailored to the capabilities of the students who are intended to enrol in them, this difficulty can be largely overcome.

(3) As important as the need may be to educate and train people to be adaptable, we also have an obligation to provide students with sufficient specialized knowledge to make them readily employable. Without adequate post high school training facilities, both public and private, and in the absence of a greater willingness on the part of individual employers to do more training themselves, the high schools have been increasingly burdened with this responsibility. If we are to require the secondary schools to concentrate on broad vocational preparation—as is suggested by the previous objective—then significant changes will have to be made at the post high school level.[1]

Even then, however, the problem will not be an easy one to resolve. The Report of the Special Committee of the Senate on Manpower and Employment was very cogent in stating the complex nature of the challenge which confronts us in this regard:

> In order to be effective, vocational and technical training should be carefully planned and must be based on the most reliable estimates of future job requirements. However, it is important to bear in mind that forecasting is fallible, and that even under the best conditions one cannot hope to predict precisely the skills which will be in demand five, ten, or twenty years from now. In view of this, emphasis should be placed on flexibility. As much as possible people should be given the sort of basic training that will permit them to move with the times. Specialization is essential and unavoidable in the modern economy, but a sound balance must be achieved between specialization and adaptability. *This is easy to say and much more difficult to*

---

[1] By post high school level we mean to include all types of programs and facilities which are designed to better equip students who have left the secondary schools for work, whether or not the students involved have successfully completed a terminal course at the high school level.

implement. Nevertheless, this should be one of the guiding principles in any programme of vocational training. We must prepare people for a world of work that is continually in evolution. (Emphasis added.)[1]

This Committee does not suggest that what is embodied in the later sections of this Report provides the final answer to this dilemma. The problem of devising an educational and training system which combines both broadly-based training and the acquisition of a specific trade or skill is one which will always be present. Although we believe that our many proposals in this area will provide part of the answer to this problem, we recognize that only time and experience will yield a more complete solution.

(4) Associated with the previous point is the need to begin to think much more earnestly about education and training as a continuing process. To do otherwise will be to underestimate the degree of skill and the amount of adjustment which is likely to be required of our labour force in the future. For many of our workers education and training may virtually have to become "a cradle-to-the-grave proposition". Over time it is bound to become increasingly unrealistic to expect finished products from our schools, whether at the high school or post high school level. As a result we will no longer be able to accept the securing of employment as a terminal point in a worker's education. Instead it will merely entail a change in method, orientation and emphasis in this regard.

The need for continuity in our educational and training programs has been adequately expressed in the following terms:

> Our recommendation goes in an entirely different direction: It may sound platitudinous, but what we are calling for is a new lifelong learning, based on our conviction, on our knowledge that we can no longer afford, as a nation and as individuals, to learn a skill and then hope to be able to live a meaningful life and perform competently on the job on the basis of that skill.
>
> Within the memory of most of us in this room today there was a day when a journeyman carpenter could hope to acquire a basic body of skills which he could then use for the rest of his life. The physician of the recent past was able to acquire his education without having to work too hard at updating his skills. Teachers could hope

---

[1] The Senate of Canada, *Report of the Special Committee of the Senate on Manpower and Employment,* op. cit., p. 8.

to master their subject matter and teach the next generation on the strength of this knowledge. As teachers and educators, we always did talk about the need for lifelong learning, and as a nation we are convinced of the advantages of additional information to be acquired for a more meaningful life for all of us, but this was almost in the nature of an extravagance, of something desirable, of a luxury rather than a necessity.

The meaning of the new industrial revolution is that this extravagance of former years has become a new imperative. To survive as productive members of our society and even to enjoy the opportunities offered by the promise of additional leisure will require additional knowledge and life-long learning. It seems certain that all of us, whether we work with our hands, with words, or with ideas, will have to learn two or three more separate sets of skills.[1]

(5) In keeping with the spirit of the previous objectives, we must provide a wide range of facilities at the adult level to meet the upgrading and training needs of special groups of individuals. At the very least, this must include special programs for each of the following purposes:

    (i) Salvaging drop-outs and enhancing their employability;
    (ii) Training unemployed workers who have obsolete skills or who are relatively unskilled;
    (iii) Upgrading employed persons who otherwise would be displaced from their jobs;
    (iv) Facilitating the integration of immigrants into constructive employment;
    (v) Rehabilitating inmates of penal institutions;
    (vi) Rehabilitating disabled and handicapped persons

(6) To take full advantage of the comprehensive educational and training system outlined above, we must place much more emphasis on manpower research—especially with regard to occupational forecasting—and we must establish competent counselling services. In the absence of either or both of these "staff" functions, we will continue to run an unduly large risk of channelling people into trades and occupations which are likely to become obsolete soon after they enter or re-enter the labour force.

---
[1] Dr. George E. Arnstein, Assistant Director of the U.S. National Education Association "Special Project on the Educational Implications of Automation", "Automation—Challenge for Education", *The Industrial Arts Teacher* (May-June, 1961) p. 21.

(7) To ensure efficient utilization of our human resources, everything possible will have to be done to provide every student with as much education and training as he is capable of effectively absorbing. To place undue obstacles in the way of the qualified student, especially at the higher levels of learning, is to countenance an economic waste which we can ill afford. Moreover, as more and more skill and knowledge is demanded of our labour force, equality of opportunity will increasingly become equated with equality of access to the higher forms of education and training. On both economic and social grounds, therefore, we must be prepared to devote increasing assistance to the children of lower income families in their pursuit of higher education and training.

(8) Finally, and perhaps most important of all, there is the need to think in terms of a much more co-ordinated approach to education and training. We can no longer afford the luxury of permitting each of the various facets of our educational and training system to go its own way. We must begin to think in terms of an integrated approach to these matters.

There are least three major reasons for emphasizing this point. In the first place there is the obvious danger that without co-ordination bottlenecks will invariably develop which can only be overcome with undue haste or prolonged delay. In this connection there is the related obligation to ensure that our outlays for education and training are expended as efficiently as possible. Thirdly, there is the need to see that the whole educational and training system is so structured as to permit ready progress from one level of proficiency to another. For these and other reasons, we can no longer afford an unplanned approach to education and training.

PART II

A BRIEF REVIEW OF ONTARIO'S PRESENT VOCATIONAL EDUCATION AND TRAINING SYSTEM[1]

THE task of this Committee has been rendered less difficult by a number of recent developments in the Province. These developments have evidenced an awareness of many of the problems discussed above and a willingness to do something about them. What is even more impressive is the healthy degree of flexibility which has developed among many of our prominent educators.

Among these recent developments, none is of greater significance than the introduction of the "Robarts Plan" into the secondary schools. This Plan involves a multi-stream system structured so as to appeal to the variety of interests, aptitudes and abilities found among different students. There will be three major streams: Science, Technology and Trades; Business and Commerce; and Arts and Science, each with four and five year programs. Each of the five year programs is designed to prepare students for university. Four-year graduates, on the other hand, will be qualified to go on to other post high school institutions of learning, to enter apprenticeship or to seek immediate employment. For students unable to cope with a four or five year program, special one and two year courses will be offered in a variety of occupational subjects. Ample provision is being made to ensure that no one will be permanently frozen into a particular stream or into a particular program within any stream.

One of the most impressive things about the Plan is its intended objective of raising the status and prestige of the vocational streams to that of the traditional academic streams. In so doing, and by offering on a more widespread basis a variety of integrated programs

---

[1]This Part of the Report is not intended to embody a detailed résumé of all of the activites in Ontario in the field of vocational education and training. Instead, it is designed to put our overall effort in this regard into reasonably sharp perspective. More detail on specific aspects of the program will follow in the next part of the Report.

which combine the teaching of both trade or office practice and academic instruction, the Plan will probably induce more students to stay in school for longer periods of time. As long as these students are enrolled in courses which are geared to their absorptive capacities and as long as the courses are designed to impart knowledge which will be useful to these students in their later lives, this is all to the good. Related to this advantage is the fact that for those students who do choose to drop out of school there will be more likelihood of their having received at least some vocational preparation. In terms of securing employment, this should provide them with some advantage over present-day drop-outs who have often been exposed to little or no technical or commercial instruction.

Also worthy of note is the work which is being done at the trade school and technical institute levels, especially in Toronto. In the Provincial Institute of Trades and in the Ryerson Institute of Technology, the Committee has found excellent examples of what can be accomplished through facilities such as these. Not only do they operate first-class day school programs but they also offer excellent evening courses.

Extension services at all levels in our educational and training system are assuming more and more importance. It is encouraging to witness the rapidly expanding enrollments in evening classes, both in Toronto and in many other centres as well. This is another area in which much has been accomplished in this Province in recent years.

In a number of other fields a great deal of progress has been made under the auspices of the Technical and Vocational Training Agreement between the Labour Department in Ottawa and the Department of Education in Ontario. Negotiated under the terms of the Federal Technical and Vocational Training Assistance Act,[1] this Agreement provides for both capital and administrative grants of between 50 and 100% from the Federal Government for various types of vocational education and training expenditures. On the capital side the Agreement provides that the Federal Government will pay 75% of all approved capital expenditures for vocational purposes which are completed and paid for by March 31, 1963. If not completed by that date (with minor exceptions), the federal contribution drops to 50%.

On the operational side the Agreement provides for the Federal Government to pay a varying share (in one case it is an absolute

---
[1] S.C. 1960-61, C.6.

amount) of approved costs at the provincial level for programs which comply with the conditions laid down in the Agreement. Included under this phase of the Agreement are the following programs:[1]

Program 1 covers those courses, given as an integral part of high school education, in which at least one-half of the school time is devoted to technical, commercial and other vocational subjects or courses designed to prepare students for entry into employment by developing occupational qualifications or to prepare students for further training in technological fields. Federal assistance for this purpose is allotted to the provinces on a quota basis and in the case of Ontario represents a nominal portion of total expenditures.

Program 2 provides for a federal contribution of 50% of the costs involved in the post-high school training of qualified technicians. This is applicable to courses such as those offered by institutes of technology.

Program 3 provides for a federal contribution of 50% of the costs involved in programs which provide pre-employment training, upgrading or retraining for persons over the compulsory school attendance age who have left elementary school and who require such training to develop or increase occupational competence or skills.

Program 4 provides that the Federal Government will share 50% to 75% of the costs involved in certain types of training in co-operation with industry. It encompasses any program designed to upgrade or retrain employees, including supervisory training courses.

Program 5 provides that the Federal Government will pay 75% of the costs involved, in training or retraining unemployed workers unless the number of training days attained in the Province drops below a specified quota. In the latter event the federal share drops to 50%.

Program 6 provides for a federal contribution of 50% of the costs involved in training disabled workers.

Program 7 provides for a federal contribution of 50% of the costs involved in programs designed to provide training for occupationally competent persons in the art or science of teaching, supervising, or in the administration of technical or vocational training programs at all levels whether in industry, in vocational schools, or in institutes.

Program 8 provides that the Federal Government will pay up to 100% of the costs involved in training persons for the federal government service.

In addition to these programs there is a ninth program which provides for federal grants for university purposes and there is a separate agreement with the Provincial Department of Labour which provides

---

[1]Only the basic principles applying to each of these programs are outlined in the following summaries. Reference should be made to the actual text of the Federal-Provincial Agreement for a more complete description of the programs.

for a federal contribution of 50% of the major operational costs borne by the province in connection with approved apprenticeship programs.

Between the Robarts Plan and the various programs for which federal assistance may be realized, Ontario has an excellent framework within which to structure its overall educational and training system. The challenge is to determine how best to utilize this framework. Although the Province has gone a long way towards meeting this challenge, there is still much to be done. This is reflected in the spotty nature of our existing programs. We have an excellent vocational high school here, a fine technical institute there, a new adult training centre somewhere else, and so on. The varying quality and the unbalanced geographical dispersion of these facilities suggests that our approach in the past has often been haphazard. Co-ordination has been lacking and common standards have not been developed.

Thus, while much progress has been made in the Province in recent years, there are gaps in our overall system which require immediate attention. In addition to this there are various facets of the existing programs which deserve thorough examination. The state of the present apprenticeship program, for example, is such as to command careful scrutiny. Similarly, there is an obvious need to re-examine our efforts in a number of other areas. Among other things which receive critical attention in the next part of this Report are: other (non-apprenticeship) forms of training in industry, supervisory training and management development, and special programs designed to facilitate the integration of immigrants into constructive employment. In each of these areas and in the other areas discussed in the next parts of this Report, something is already being done in this province. In many cases, however, not enough progress has yet been made.

Especially disturbing is the lack of adequate vocational counselling and the absence of any kind of organized manpower research. Without these services it stands to reason that we cannot allocate our funds as wisely as we should and we will not be able to advise and channel students as effectively as we might.

All of these deficiencies must obviously be corrected if we are to bring our vocational education and training system fully up to date. Once having done so there will still have to be a continuing audit of the overall system. Only by this means can we begin to keep it as effective as possible for any length of time.

PART III

COMMENTS AND RECOMMENDATIONS WITH REGARD TO SPECIFIC FACETS OF OUR EXISTING EDUCATIONAL AND TRAINING SYSTEM

IMPLICIT in the overall objectives set forth in a previous section of this Report are a number of specific thoughts and suggestions with regard to the present state of our educational and training system. In the remainder of the Report we outline our many comments and recommendations in a more specific fashion.

THE ROBARTS PLAN—SOME ADDITIONAL OBSERVATIONS

Although we are in basic agreement with the changes which are now taking place in many of our secondary school systems under the name of the Robarts Plan, we do have certain reservations which we would like to bring out.

(i) One of the matters which concerns us most is the stigma which still pertains to vocational education in this Province—both among the public at large and, more seriously, among academic educators and administrators as well. In many communities this attitude is still reflected in a long-standing tradition of using the technical and commercial courses as a form of dumping ground for poor students, discipline problems and others unwanted by academic teachers. Over the years this has had a very detrimental effect upon the status and reputation of the vocational courses. While it is encouraging to note that several outstanding vocational schools have emerged in various centres in this Province, they are still fighting an uphill battle. Until this battle is won the vocational courses and thus the whole concept which underlies the Robarts Plan will be at a serious disadvantage.

We would therefore urge that the Department of Education step up its efforts—among educators as well as the general public—to build up the status and prestige of the non-academic streams in the new multi-stream system.

(ii) Closely tied in with the need to build up the status and prestige of vocational education is the need to make the general public more conversant with the overall thinking which lies behind the new system. It is obvious that the whole purpose of the Plan will fail in the absence of adequate public understanding of the advantages of the multi-stream system. While much has been done to make the public more aware of these advantages, it is our belief that there is still a great deal to be done. In large measure this is mainly a public relations matter. In addition, however, it comes down to the need for much more comprehensive vocational counselling, a matter to which we shall return at more length later in this report.

(iii) Another matter which has gravely concerned this Committee pertains to the relative advantages which are likely to accrue to students in various parts of this Province as a result of the Robarts Plan. The nature of the multi-stream system is such as to demand a large student body in order to make it feasible to offer a complete range of alternatives. While the large concentration of students in major urban centres is likely to permit full realization of the intent of the Plan in these communities, such is less likely to be the case where the student population is scattered over a wide territory. To facilitate the necessary degree of specialization in these areas it may require even further consolidation of school districts than we have witnessed in the past. Special grants may also have to be considered to assist local boards of education which are confronted with this type of situation. If these measures do not suffice we may eventually have to turn over more responsibility to the Province for the provision of secondary education.

(iv) Related to the foregoing point is the need to strengthen our agricultural options in rural areas of the Province. Although there has been a gradual but persistent movement of labour away from the farm to the city, the need is no less vital today than it has been in the past to provide first rate vocational training in agricultural subjects. Indeed, with the technology of agriculture changing as rapidly as it is, this need will probably become even more pressing in the future.

At the same time, however, because so many of our rural youth will not find permanent employment in agriculture, ample provision must be made for training in vocational subjects which are likely to prove useful for those who expect to migrate to urban areas.

(v) The increased holding power of the schools depends in large measure upon the number and variety of new vocational options. While the Robarts Plan does involve a considerable expansion in the number and variety of such options, we venture to suggest that we may eventually have to move even farther in this regard. As we understand it, the four and five year vocational streams will only permit the student to devote about 50% of his time to shop or commercial work and to directly related academic instruction.[1] Whether this will prove a sufficient inducement to retain the interest of those who are not academically inclined but do have the capacity to absorb four or five years of vocationally oriented schooling remains to be seen. To increase the practical content of the vocational streams would be to lessen the opportunity for graduates of these courses to proceed to higher education. Despite this disadvantage it may still be necessary to consider such a modification at least with regard to the four-year programs. As an alternative it might some day prove worthwhile to think in terms of a program which would lie somewhere between the two-year occupational and the four-year vocational courses.

(vi) Our sixth comment on the Robarts Plan relates to the need for more imagination on the part of local boards of education when they are establishing new vocational programs. While a number of school boards have evidenced a good deal of initiative in developing programs geared to future employment needs in their localities, others have shown little or no such initiative. Instead they have settled for establishing a number of courses in what by now might be termed "the standard trades". Scores of vocational school projects have been approved and developed which only offer training in automotives,

---

On the average this 50% is split up approximately on a 40-60 basis between shop or commercial work and related academic instruction.

electricity, metalworking, woodworking, drafting and typing. This is likely to leave us with a rash of partially trained young people in a very limited number of occupations.

Not all of the blame for this state of affairs resides at the local level. There has been less direction and guidance from the Provincial Department of Education than might have been expected. As the one body capable of approaching this question from an overall provincial point of view, it should have attempted to prevent these trends from emerging on such a wide scale. Although handicapped by the unduly rigid time limits laid down under the Federal Provincial Agreement, the Department could have given more direction and guidance.

In the future everything possible will have to be done to avoid a repetition of this sort of thing. To begin with an intensive study should be made of the procedures adopted by those communities which appear to have shown the most imagination in assessing their future manpower needs and in developing appropriate vocational programs.

(vii) If more emphasis is to be placed on broad vocational preparation in the secondary schools—as we think it should—there is less need to be distressed by the fact that so many of our new vocational schools have concentrated on the same limited range of courses. In the long run—as was suggested in the second of our overall objectives—it is our belief that less emphasis should be placed on specialized vocational training at the secondary school level.

For the present, however, we are forced to rely on the secondary schools to do a good deal of our specialized training. Until more facilities are available at the post-high school level this is bound to remain the case and it is unfortunate that during that period we may find ourselves turning out too many potential specialists in a limited range of fields.

(viii) Our final comment concerns the relative emphasis which should be placed on different courses within the vocational field. In the future it is our view that the demand for white collar and service workers will grow disproportionately faster than the demand for blue collar workers. Exploratory work on projecting manpower requirements carried out by the Department of Labour in Ottawa suggests that a substantial and growing proportion of the new jobs which are likely to emerge in the next decade are going to fall within the white collar and service category.

Excluding the white collar technician and professional, this is likely to be reflected in a tremendous upsurge in our demand for stenographic, sales and administrative personnel, relative to the traditional blue collar occupations. If this is true—and the on-going trend in the aggregate national data certainly suggests that it is—then more and more of our attention on the vocational side of education will have to be focused on the Business and Commerce stream. In the long run it will also almost certainly tend to increase our requirements for those with a solid academic background.

AN EXPANDING ROLE FOR THE TRADE SCHOOLS

The Committee has been very impressed by the work of the Provincial Institute of Trades and the new Provincial Institue of Automotive and Allied Trades. We thus welcome the addition of the new trade schools at Ottawa, London and Sault Ste. Marie. Even if the role of the trade schools is largely confined to the provision of classroom instruction in conjunction with apprenticeship, we would expect that all of these facilities will eventually be taxed to capacity. This reflects our belief that if our recommendations concerning the apprenticeship programs are fully implemented, there will be a substantial increase in the number of indentured apprentices in this Province. In addition to this there will almost certainly be a tendency to extend the amount of time devoted to full-time trade school instruction during the apprenticeship period. For both of these reasons we are confident that ample use will be made of the trade schools in the future, if only in relation to their role in connection with the apprenticeship system.

It is not our belief that the trade schools should be confined to the latter role. We would suggest that they be employed for many other purposes as well. There is no reason, for example, why they should not be available for salvaging drop-outs by equipping them with skills in the less demanding trades and occupations. In a like fashion they should be prepared to offer pre-apprenticeship courses to bring those lacking sufficient standards up to the point where they can qualify for apprenticeship training itself. In some cases the trade schools should also be available to supplement local board of education resources in the training of unemployed workers. Where employers set about to upgrade their existing work force, the trade schools should likewise be prepared to supplement other local facilities if the employer himself is not equipped to provide the related classroom and shop instruction which may be required. For individuals who wish to upgrade themselves the trade schools should continue to offer both full-time and part-time evening programs in any fields where there is sufficient demand for this sort of opportunity. To avoid competing with local board of education offerings, both groups should attempt to confine themselves to those areas where they have a comparative advantage.

Looking to the future we would reiterate our belief that the trade schools will have to be made available to train graduates of the vocational schools in specialized skills needed for immediate employment. This is in keeping with our conclusion that changes in the labour force are taking place so rapidly that we must avoid over-specialization in our education and training at too early a stage. As the secondary schools begin to concentrate on broad vocational preparation designed to facilitate adaptability, the trade schools will have to carry more of the burden for specialized pre-employment training.

It will thus be necessary for the government to establish more trade schools and to disperse them more widely across the Province. Wider dispersal is particularly important in order to offset the comparative disadvantage of sparsely populated regions that cannot provide a broad range of vocational options at the secondary school level. In multiplying its efforts at the trade school level, the government would probably be wise to give some consideration to the possibility of a new name for these schools. Such a name should be more in keeping with the multi-functional nature of the training which is now being offered in these institutions.

OUR GROWING NEED FOR TECHNICIANS—
THE ROLE OF THE TECHNICAL INSTITUTES

In assessing the information which is now available on our future manpower requirements, nothing has impressed this Committee more than the growing demand for all manner of technicians. Since the war we have relied very heavily on immigration to satisfy our requirements in this area. In addition to this a number of large firms have established their own programs for meeting their need for technicians.

To supplement these sources the government established the Haileybury School of Mines (Haileybury) and the Ryerson Institute of Technology (Toronto) shortly after World War II. Since that time additional institutes have been established at Ottawa, Hamilton, Windsor, and Kirkland Lake. Expansion of all of these facilities has taken place at a rapid rate. They are now capable of enrolling 5,000 full-time students and are providing part-time evening instruction to approximately the same number.

Of all of the programs we have considered we cannot think of any more important than the training of technicians. Modern technology requires a vast complement of highly qualified personnel to man and maintain the new equipment. This is one area which we neglect at our peril. Unless we produce an adequate supply of technicians, we will find ourselves at a serious disadvantage in the technological world in which we live.

Because of this the Committee feels that we must be prepared to greatly intensify our efforts at this level. Our main reliance will have to be placed on full-time day courses but this should not lead us to neglect other possibilities. Where individual firms or industries show a willingness to cooperate, day-or-block release and sandwich courses must also be introduced. Under a day-or-block release system the classes are made up of students who spend most of their time training and working on the job. They are released for a day a week or for a longer period in order to obtain intensive classroom instruction. An extension of this principle is the sandwich course whereby students spend one-half the year at school and one-half on the job for a period of from two to four years.

We would also urge that as much use as possible be made of the technical institutes to offer night extension courses, either to individuals in general or in conjunction with programs offered by various private organizations. The service which is now being rendered in this regard is most commendable. We suggest that it be extended wherever it seems practical to do so.

In urging a stepped-up effort to train technicians in this Province, we are not unmindful of the fact that many graduate engineers are presently doing technical work. This has led us to believe that we are perhaps graduating too many university trained engineers relative to the number of technicians which are being turned out. This was borne out by the testimony of the representative of the Association of Professional Engineers of Ontario (Proceedings p. 1593):

> There is a question in my mind whether or not a large number of people channelled to university should not be channelled to technician. [*sic*]

What this seems to suggest is that some thought should be given to curtailing further expansion of our engineering schools until we realize a better balance between our needs at this level and those at the technician levels. We would not entertain any such curtailment, however, of our post-graduate engineering school programs. There should probably be a continuing expansion of our efforts at that level.

In the course of our investigations it has been brought to our attention that the Ryerson Institute of Technology is gradually narrowing the difference between its standards and those of our engineering schools. While there may be a need for at least one senior institute of technology in this Province, we question whether Ryerson should aspire to anything beyond this. To go beyond this point would further compound the existing imbalance between our supply of technicians and engineers.

THE UNIVERSITY CRISIS

Although we have deliberately excluded the universities from our general terms of reference, we have decided that we would be remiss in our responsibilities if we failed to make some reference to the critical problem before us at the university level. The latest estimates available suggest that university enrolment in Ontario can be expected to rise by about 300% in the next decade. This is based on the assumption that no more than the present proportion of those who successfully complete Grade XIII will go on to university. If it is decided to provide even more Grade XIII graduates with the opportunity to attend university, the numbers involved will obviously tend to increase at an even more rapid rate.

Suffice it to say that unless much more aid is rapidly forthcoming to the universities, thousands of students who would today qualify for university will not be afforded that opportunity ten years hence. This is a possibility that cannot be countenanced if we are to produce a sufficient amount of high level talent to sustain a satisfactory measure of economic and social progress.

APPRENTICESHIP IN THE BUILDING TRADES

For the training of workers in the building trades apprenticeship has been the traditional vehicle. Under this system workers are indentured to employers for periods ranging from two to five years. During that time, the bulk of their training is provided on the job. Over the years, however, on-the-job training has been increasingly supplemented by related classroom instruction.

Although there are alternative ways in which tradesmen in the building trades can be developed, this Committee is convinced that a good apprenticeship program is potentially the most effective. Unfortunately, the apprenticeship program in the building trades in this Province has not been as effective as it should have been. Except in one or two of the crafts the number of apprentices successfully completing the program has amounted to a small fraction of replacement let alone any need for expansion. Something radical must be done to correct this situation.

(i) In order to build up the apprenticeship program, more incentive must be provided to encourage young workers to enter into it. This can only be done by affording those who successfully complete an apprenticeship program due and proper recognition for their accomplishment.

(ii) To this end it is our view that compulsory certification should be applied to all trades which can be expected to benefit from it. Where adopted this will ensure that only those who have proven their competency to practice a given trade will be permitted to engage in it. This will not only act as an incentive for those considering a career in the building trades but will also serve to protect the interests of the public by assuring them a minimum standard of competence.[1]

There is the danger that compulsory certification could be employed as part of a general scheme to restrict numbers and take advantage of the public. It will be up to those government officials who are closest to the apprenticeship program to guard against any such possibility.

We must also insist that compulsory certification not be applied to

---

[1] It is to be noted that compulsory certification is now in effect in the motor vehicle trades and in hairdressing.

any trade unless it is accompanied by legislation or regulations consistent with the following recommendations.

(iii) Where compulsory certification is put into effect in any trade, earnest consideration should be given to the possibility of classifying appropriate journeyman-level specialties and/or varying grades of proficiency within the trade. The use of both types of designations should be made mandatory except in those trades where they prove to be absolutely unnecessary or completely unworkable.

In so far as the designation of different specialties is concerned this should present no real problem. Even today when a contractor requests men from a union it is common practice for him to specify the kind of work for which he requires them. The business agent normally knows which of the available men are best qualified for different types of work and sends them out accordingly. Additional formalization in this regard should present no major difficulty. This is exactly what is done in the motor vehicle trades at the present time and it appears to be working out very satisfactorily.

Much more controversial, we realize, is the suggestion that certificates denoting differing levels of competency be issued. Just as there are several terminal points in the new vocational high school program and various levels of proficiency within the technician category in this Province, likewise should the same general principle be applied to the building trades. It is our belief that in virtually all of the trades at least two levels of proficiency are demanded. There should be a basic minimum standard established in each of the trades as well as the traditional journeyman standard.

In the face of the skill dilution which is being brought about by technological changes and other developments in the industry, we cannot believe that every tradesman in the building trades has to become a fully-trained journeyman in order to make a useful contribution. The very fact that the unions have taken into their membership workers who have not gone through an apprenticeship program or otherwise evidenced such a degree of competency attests to the validity of this assertion. It would be economically wasteful to impose an unnecessarily high standard on all those wishing to make their livelihood in the construction industry. This point was made abundantly clear by a reference which was made to recent developments in the carpentry trade by one of the representatives of the **Ontario Federation of Labour** (Proceedings, p. 588):

> The facts of the matter are that supply and demand have made the carpentry trade today exactly what it is, that you need about seventy or eighty per cent hammer and saw men and about ten or twenty per cent skilled carpenters.

Although this trend is less apparent in other trades, it is present in varying degrees in all of them.

The imposition of one unnecessarily high standard in each of the different trades would also be grossly unfair to the many thousands in our labour force who may be quite capable of mastering certain basic elements of a trade but who may not be sufficiently endowed to successfully complete an entire apprenticeship program.

Because of these considerations we urge that at least two types of certificates be issued in the various trades. The first would be at the journeyman level and would indicate those aspects of the trade in which the journeyman was particularly qualified. The second certificate would be issued to those able to master the basic elements of a trade but who are unable to attain a full journeyman standard. The ability to perform one or two specialized tasks should not be deemed sufficient to qualify for the junior certificate. This would not be enough to ensure such individuals any degree of employment continuity. Instead, a basic knowledge of the fundamentals of the trade must be insisted upon. This would permit such individuals to shift about readily from one type of relatively simple and specialized task to another. As distinct from the journeyman, however, they would not be competent to deal with the more difficult and advanced elements of the trade. To protect the legitimate interests of the fully-trained journeyman, care would have to be taken to ensure that junior tradesmen were not permitted to do the skilled types of work for which they had not proven competent.

Union resistance to these proposals is to be expected. While they have urged upon us the adoption of compulsory certification, they have indicated opposition to the designation of varying levels of competency. We agree entirely with them and with others who appeared before the Committee that the only way to overcome the deficiencies in the present program is to introduce compulsory certification. But to insist on one relatively high level of proficiency would be uneconomic and unfair. We have therefore recommended a graded system of certification. This would not only serve to protect the public but would also be beneficial to the great majority of the workers involved. It would provide tradesmen with the recognition they deserve and would eliminate the kind of back-door entry into the trades which has done so much harm in the past to the development of a qualified work force.

(iv) Where graded certification is put into effect, training for the junior levels of certification should take the form of a modified version of the journeyman apprenticeship program. Where possible it should embrace roughly the same amount of fundamental knowledge as is required of the journeyman in the first half of his apprenticeship program. This would be desirable in order to facilitate the gradual acquisition of further knowledge and skill sufficient to permit those with minimum qualifications eventually to move on up to full journeyman status. It is to be emphasized, however, that the accumulation of the additional knowledge and skill required to make such a move would probably have to be largely acquired off the job. In so far as it was permitted on the job it would have to be carefully regulated. Otherwise it would interfere with the normal apprenticeship program for full-fledged journeymen and would also tend to cut down on the work properly reserved for such journeymen.

Although we anticipate that a number of those who originally decided to qualify for a junior certificate might some day seek to move beyond that level, we do not feel that this should necessarily be expected of the majority of these individuals. For this reason it might be wise to specify less demanding educational requirements for those who do not intend to go beyond the minimum level of qualification. Should they later decide to strive for the higher level of competence, it would then be up to them to make up the necessary academic requirements.

(v) When introducing compulsory certification in any trade, consideration will have to be given to the interests of those who are already practicing the trade. Except for those who have successfully completed an apprenticeship program registered with the Department of Labour, there will be the need to establish the competency of those now in the trade. In order to be fair to these individuals, a waiting-period of up to four or five years should be allowed, during which they would be permitted to practice in the trade while at the same time bringing their proficiency up to the necessary level. Since many of these workers may not be able to attain a full journeyman standard during that period this is another reason for favouring the concept of graded certification.

(vi) Having implemented a compulsory certification scheme, the government would then have some obligation to see that an adequate number were flowing into the various trades. At the very least this would seem to require much more attention to publicity. A great deal needs to be done to make the general public more aware of the advantages of apprenticeship and of the pros and cons of a career in one of the building trades. Particular emphasis should be placed on the need to acquaint vocational counsellors with these matters.

(vii) In addition to this, more pre-apprenticeship training for drop-outs and unemployed workers should be made available. Such courses should not be allowed to impinge unduly on the apprenticeship programs themselves but should concentrate upon providing potential apprentices with the necessary academic qualifications or the equivalent.

(viii) Because of the number that may be expected to enter apprenticeship via the pre-apprenticeship route and because of the fact that many potential apprentices do not see the value of apprenticeship until several years after they have left school, it stands to reason that the present age limit of twenty-one cannot be tolerated. The suggestion has been made that it be lifted to twenty-five. We do not believe that this is sufficient. To our way of thinking no such artificial restriction as age should be placed in the way of a man who wishes to become an apprentice and who is able to find an employer who is willing to take him on in that capacity. The latter is likely to prove an obstacle enough by itself. We would also suggest that to the extent that the age limit has been maintained in order to restrict entry into the trades the same protection will in part be afforded by the introduction of compulsory certification. As the representative of the International

Brotherhood of Electrical Workers said during his appearance before the Committee (Proceedings, pp. 470-7):

> We have clarified that point, and they agreed if it was compulsory certification the age limit would not be necessary. I cannot think why the age limit should remain on if we have certification.

As to the argument that the older man will not be able to live on the income of an apprentice we believe that this decision is up to him.

(ix) In addition to those who are likely to flow into apprenticeship from special pre-apprenticeship training programs, there are many others who are likely to choose apprenticeship after completing four or five years of secondary school. In connection with these potential apprentices there is the need to see that they receive adequate credit for the progress which they have made while in school. As the Ontario Federation of Labour stressed (Proceedings, p. 558):

> To encourage young people to remain in the secondary school training program, it is advisable to allow time credit on an apprenticeship program for successful completion of a regular school course.

Because of the varying standards which presently prevail in the secondary schools across this Province we do not believe it wise or possible to provide for any sort of a blanket credit system—at least for the time being. Instead, we would suggest that in each of the various trades an appropriate series of tests be devised—both practical and theoretical—to determine how much credit in the apprenticeship program should be granted to individual students leaving the secondary schools. We must insure that every student receives the credit he deserves as a result of his previous work.

(x) As a further extension of the latter principle it is our belief that no man should be barred from securing certification in any trade simply because he has not gone through apprenticeship. Although we would not expect that many individuals would be able to qualify for a trade without going through apprenticeship such a possibility should not be ruled out. Regardless of how a skill has been acquired it should be subject to public recognition. Appropriate tests should be devised for this purpose and the trade schools should be prepared to administer them.

(xi) To ensure that employers are willing to take a sufficient number of apprentices to provide for the future needs of the industry is most difficult. The simple answer would be to require that every contractor maintain a specified ratio of apprentices to the number of journeymen in his employ. Short of this it might be desirable to levy a special payroll tax on all employers in each of the trades to finance the apprenticeship system. Such funds could be used to assist those contractors who were willing to carry their share of apprenticeship training.

Another possibility—and the one which appeals to us most—avoids the blatant aspects of compulsion. If no firm was allowed to bid on any government construction project unless it normally employed an appropriate complement of apprentices, this would certainly go a long way towards building up an adequate supply of qualified journeymen for the future. If this did not prove a sufficient inducement we could then fall back on either or both of the previous possibilities.

(xii) Administrative responsibility for the apprenticeship program in the building trades has been vested in the Department of Labour ever since the program was inaugurated. The role of the Department of Education has been confined to the provision of related classroom instruction in accordance with specifications worked out jointly between the two departments.

This division of authority has given rise to a good deal of friction and has permitted both departments to attempt to shift the blame to the other for deficiencies in the present program. How best to resolve this situation is a problem which has plagued this Committee since its inception. While we cannot prescribe a clear-cut solution, we can point out what the two most practical alternatives are. Which approach is adopted must be a top-level decision and once made must receive the full support of all concerned.

(a) If the decision is made to transfer complete responsibility for the apprenticeship program to one or other of the two departments then there is only one choice which can be made. Because of the role which the trade schools should play in other facets of manpower training besides apprenticeship, we believe that it would be most unwise to turn over the administration of these schools to the Department of Labour. This rules out the possibility of the latter taking over complete control of the apprenticeship program. If a single authority is the answer then the entire responsibility for apprenticeship would have to be turned over to the Department of Education.

Logically there is much to be said for this possibility. It would bring apprenticeship under the wing of the department which now bears the responsibility for virtually all other phases of manpower training and development in this Province. It would thus facilitate the integration of the apprenticeship program into our overall system of education and training. In the long run such an integration is an absolute necessity if our manpower training and development system is to be properly planned and co-ordinated.

On the other side of the ledger, however, there is the fact that the Department of Education has not developed extensive contacts with labour and management in the construction industry. Without these contacts no successful apprenticeship program can be operated. It is also to be remembered that apprenticeship impinges upon a number of sensitive issues in the general field of union-management relations. Whether the Department of Education would be capable of coping with these questions effectively is a matter for conjecture. Since lack of union or management cooperation could easily undermine any apprenticeship program it should be obvious that these considerations should not be passed over lightly.

If in the final analysis the decision is made to turn over apprenticeship to the Department of Education two things are mandatory. In the first place it is our firm conviction that the Director and the present staff of the Apprenticeship Branch would have to be included in the transfer. This in itself would be a very effective way in which to minimize the problems which could be associated with the lack of contacts referred to above.

In the second place we would make any such transfer to the Department of Education contingent upon the apprenticeship program being administered as part of an overall industrial education program. Otherwise, the danger is that the apprenticeship program could be subverted to the purposes of those who feel that academic education comes first. To allow this to happen would be to destroy the very basis of apprenticeship. As a means of skill acquisition apprenticeship remains a method which is very much tied to on-the-job training.

While related classroom instruction is likely to become increasingly important over time, such instruction must be kept as practical and work-oriented as possible. For all of these reasons we would not recommend that apprenticeship be transferred to the Department of Education unless the essence of the changes which we later advance with regard to the administration of vocational and industrial education in the latter are adopted.

(b) Instead of the former possibility an effort could be made to strengthen the existing arrangements between the two departments. This would have the advantage of avoiding the disruption—temporary or permanent — which would inevitably result from a wholesale change in the existing division of responsibilities.

The Department of Labour has some strong claims to the apprenticeship program. It has close relations with the various unions and managements involved and is fully conversant with the labour-relations implications of apprenticeship. These are advantages which should not be minimized.

At the same time, however, there are grounds for questioning whether the Department of Labour should maintain its present position in the field of apprenticeship. Despite the above advantages apprenticeship has not prospered during its many years under the Department of Labour. The results have been quite unsatisfactory. This does not appear to be the fault of the Apprenticeship Branch itself but rather has reflected the lack of support which the Branch has received in the Department as a whole. Because the Department of Labour necessarily has a labour-relations orientation, it may well be inhibited from administering the apprenticeship program in as objective and detached a manner as is required. Unless this potential disadvantage can be overcome it may not be possible to entrust the Department of Labour with as much responsibility for apprenticeship as it has enjoyed in the past.

Whether the present division of authority can ever produce the desired results remains to be seen. Should the decision be made to maintain the existing system it is obvious that a strenuous effort will have to be made to improve the present relations between the two departments.

Unless the differences which have often characterized relations between the Apprenticeship Branch in the Department of Labour and the staff of the trade schools are eradicated, a major obstacle will remain. To the extent that the source of these difficulties lies with the Department of Labour's resistance to any form of training (outside of apprenticeship) which infringes in any way upon the apprenticeable trades, the situation can only be rectified by the Department showing a more open and less restrictive attitude. To the extent that the difficulties result from an attempt on the part of the Department of Education to inject an undue degree of academic content into trades training, the fault would seem to lie with the latter. If the existing division of authority is to be continued a high level conference of all those concerned must be convened as soon as possible to iron out the differences which exist between the two groups. Such a conference should also consider the possibility of having a Department of Education official sit as a member of the Provincial Advisory Committee(s) for the Building Trades. If steps such as these are taken it might be possible to revitalize apprenticeship in the building trades without resorting to more drastic administrative changes.

(c) More important than anything else in the effective operation of an apprenticeship program is the will to succeed on the part of all those involved. This is a factor which must be given the closest consideration when the decision is ultimately made as to what should be done to expedite the administration of the apprenticeship program in this Province. Our record to date has been anything but impressive. The challenge is to decide upon an appropriate course of action and to give it our full support.

(xiii) We would also like to advance a number of more specific recommendations with regard to apprenticeship in the building trades. The first of these pertains to the question as to whom the apprentice should be indentured. In the past, it has been the usual custom to indenture the apprentice to an individual employer. It is our feeling that it would be more appropriate to indenture the apprentice to a local joint apprenticeship committee or failing that to the appropriate branch of the government. This would facilitate transfers between individual employers and would thus reduce the risk of a layoff interrupting the planned progression of the apprentice through the entire system. It would also prove conducive to providing apprentices with more comprehensive and well-rounded on-the-job training.

(xiv) To ensure that apprentices are not exploited as a form of cheap labour, we must be prepared to do more inspection of the on-the-job side of apprenticeship. This is inescapable if we are to gain full value from our apprenticeship system.

(xv) We would also like to suggest that consideration be given to the development of a multi-trade apprenticeship program where this seems appropriate. We noted with interest the remarks of the Ontario General Contractors Association and the Toronto Construction Association in this regard (Proceedings, p. 927):

> It is conceivable that, in certain areas of the industry, such as heavy engineering, road building and house building, major economies and a greater degree of continuous employment could be derived as a result of a multi-trade apprenticeship program.

They went on to recommend that (Proceedings, p. 939):

> A composite committee, comprised of special representatives of the Apprenticeship Branch of the Department of Labour and members of organized employer groups in the industry, be formed to investigate the desirability of a multi-trade apprenticeship training program.

We endorse this proposal and suggest that where technological and other changes are tending to blur traditional craft dividing lines, it is unrealistic to conceive of avoiding some form of multi-trade training. A similar approach would also seem to be called for in small towns or in rural areas where the market is not sufficient to support qualified tradesmen in each of the various trades. We would add, however, that when a committee is established to study the implementation of such an approach, it must include representatives from the affected trade unions.

(xvi) Because technological changes and other developments are continually upsetting conditions in the building trades, the apprenticeship program should be administered in as flexible a fashion as possible. In the words of the Ontario Federation of Labour (Proceedings, p. 557):

> The actual terms of apprenticeship, the age limits, period and duration of training, should be related directly to the needs of the trade and industry, and should be continually under review. They must be modified and changed as often as conditions indicate.

This is in keeping with the spirit in which we have approached the concept of apprenticeship. The fact that something has been handled in a particular way in the past must not be allowed to keep us from adopting new policies and techniques which are more in line with modern conditions and needs.

(xvii) To avoid an undue adherence to the traditional way of doing things, some consideration should be given to the role and composition of the Provincial Advisory Committee for the Building Trades. To put it very bluntly, we feel that a higher degree of turnover among the membership of this body would be very healthy. For this reason we would suggest that those who are appointed to the Committee be appointed for limited terms and not be subject to immediate re-appointment. We would also recommend that this Committee play more of an advisory role than in the past. It is our impression that the Committee has often had an overly decisive hand in the formulation of policy. The Committee should play a strictly advisory role and the Apprenticeship Branch should not be expected to adhere to its advice unerringly. We would also suggest that more value could be derived from the use of such an approach if separate committees were established for each of the many trades.

(xviii) The use of local joint apprenticeship committees to supervise the operation of the apprenticeship program at the local level is to be encouraged. In so far as possible the employment of these committees should be governed by the same set of considerations as was suggested for the Provincial Advisory Committee(s). On the other hand, because the local committees are more operational in nature they must be approached in a somewhat different fashion. They must play less of an advisory role and be viewed more as an administrative wing of the apprenticeship program. For this reason, less turnover is probably desirable than at the Provincial level.

(xix) Whether they be union members or not, care must be taken to ensure that the individual interests of the apprentice are taken into consideration. The apprenticeship program must be administered so as not to discriminate against any workers—union or non-union.

(xx) As regards the use of the terms designated and non-designated trades, we would urge their discontinuance. A great deal of confusion surrounds their use and we feel that the need for any such distinction has more than outworn itself. In the future there should be only one basic distinction. The certified trades would be those for which a certificate would be required to practice the trade and the non-certified trades would be those for which there was no such requirement.

(xxi) Finally, we would urge that every consideration be given to the possibility of extending apprenticeship in the building trades to trades which are not now covered.

APPRENTICESHIP IN OTHER TRADES AND OCCUPATIONS
OUTSIDE OF GENERAL INDUSTRY

Aside from the building trades, apprenticeship has also been used extensively in the motor vehicle trades as well as in barbering and hairdressing. It is our view that virtually all of the recommendations we have made in connection with the building trades are equally applicable in these cases. Indeed, much of our thinking in regard to the building trades was prompted by the success which apprenticeship has enjoyed in recent years in the motor vehicle trades.

In passing we would also like to make note of the fact that the same set of recommendations would appear to be equally appropriate in the case of three other trades which were brought to our attention. Government sponsored apprenticeship training for cooks, for tool and die makers, and for the printing trades was strongly recommended to us during the course of our hearings. We feel that sympathetic consideration should be given to each of these possibilities.

In some of these occupations, it may be desirable to provide more in-school training as an alternative to on-the-job training. In the case of barbers and hairdressers, for example, it would appear to be just as effective to provide for a complete training in schools as to channel workers through an apprenticeship program. Where this is the case, both avenues should be kept open.

APPRENTICESHIP IN GENERAL INDUSTRY—THE NEED
FOR A SEPARATE AND DISTINCT APPROACH

Based on the evidence which we have been able to gather it is our opinion that far too little training of a formal nature is carried on in general industry. This is best evidenced by a study compiled by the Federal Department of Labour in Ottawa which showed that only 24% of the firms surveyed were operating any sort of formal apprenticeship program. Industry's failure to do more training has been one of the most critical reasons why more and more of the burden for specialized training has been thrust upon the secondary schools.

In our view something immediate must be done to correct this situation. There is a need to encourage greater use of apprenticeship in industry as well as more training in general. Since the scope for the effective use of apprenticeship in industry is usually confined to a relatively narrow band of maintenance tradesmen, it follows that greater emphasis should be placed on other types of training, at least for the present. It must be recognized, however, that as the demand for skilled tradesmen and technicians picks up in industry, relative to semi-skilled and unskilled workers, increasing reliance will have to be placed on apprenticeship-type methods of training. For this reason we shall devote more attention to this aspect of training in industry than to less formalized methods.

With regard to the use of apprenticeship in general industry, we feel that the government must avoid overplaying its hand. Unlike the situation in the building or motor vehicle trades, there is a greater need in general industry to tailor apprenticeship programs to the needs of particular firms or industries. It would be most unrealistic, for example, to attempt to develop a general apprenticeship program for machinists which would be equally applicable to all types of manufacturing. For this reason it seems desirable to permit firms as much leeway as possible in the development of their individual programs.

By and large we have been most impressed by the quality of those programs which have been brought to our attention. Their one common defect relates to the lack of any general standard which can be readily applied to them. Outside of the individual firm there is often very little known about the quality of their apprenticeship program. From the point of view of the individual firm this may be perfectly desirable since it reduces the likelihood of their being raided by other firms who have similar needs but do not do their own training. From the point of view of the successful apprentice, however, and from the point of view of society at large, this is very shortsighted. It is unfair to the apprentice because it reduces the marketability and thus the value of his newly acquired skill. It is also inefficient since it detracts from a more economic allocation of labour within the economy as a whole. If we are to employ our human resources as effectively as possible we must develop as much knowledge within our labour markets as we can. Only in this way can we hope to ensure that all workers move to the place of employment where they receive the highest rate of return and thus contribute most to the advancement of the economy.

(i) To partially rectify this situation, we recommend that the appropriate authorities draw up minimum standards applicable to various types of apprenticeship in general industry and that they provide a Provincial seal of approval to be affixed to those company certificates which are awarded under programs which meet those standards. At the very least such standards should include specifications as to the desired length of particular types of apprenticeship programs and the minimum amounts of related classroom instruction which should be required. In addition, no Provincial stamp of approval should be offered in the absence of periodic field trips designed to check on the calibre of the on-the-job training provided under particular programs. Such investigations should not be viewed as policing actions but rather as little more than general inspection tours. By no means should any attempt be made to dictate the detailed contents of individual company programs.

(ii) Where feasible special standards appropriate to the apprenticeable trades in particular industries should be worked out on an industry-wide basis. This would make possible common use of related classroom instruction and common examinations and would obviously have other advantages as well.

(iii) Multi-trade apprenticeship standards appropriate to the skill-mix requirements of different types of industrial maintenance work should also be worked out wherever practical.

(iv) We would also suggest that where firms are not large enough to maintain their own apprenticeship programs, they should be encouraged to join in cooperative undertakings with other employers. The government should do everything possible to foster a number of experiments along these lines.

(v) Every encouragement should be given to individual firms and industries to operate apprenticeship programs in compliance with the minimum standards laid down at the Provincial level. Consideration should be given to some form of financial reimbursement to those firms which meet such standards. Otherwise they are likely to become discouraged if their competitors do not carry their fair share of training in the industry and rely instead upon raiding those who do. Any such reimbursement should be modest but should be sufficiently large to provide some concrete incentive to individual firms to turn out as many skilled personnel as possible.

(vi) To provide us with a continuing inventory of the number of apprenticeship programs operating in general industry in the Province, we urge that it be made mandatory to register such programs with the appropriate authorities. Compulsory registration should in no way be used to interfere in the internal operation of such programs but should simply be employed to give us some idea, on a year to year basis, of the number of skilled workers that are being turned out under different auspices throughout the Province. Such an inventory will be essential if we are to be able to undertake any sort of intelligent assessment of our manpower training and development needs in the years ahead.

(vii) To assist in implementing the above proposals, there should be established a Provincial Advisory Committee for Apprenticeship in General Industry. Such a committee should be composed of a cross section of labour and management representatives in the field of manufacturing. The committee should function in much the same fashion as the existing provincial advisory committee for the automotive trades.

(viii) As sufficient local interest develops, similar committees should be established at that level. Where there are active chapters of the Ontario Industrial Education Council these could easily serve as the nuclei for the type of committees which we have in mind. Where practical, it might be desirable to indenture apprentices to such committees rather than to individual firms.

OTHER FORMS OF TRAINING IN GENERAL INDUSTRY[1]

Aside from apprenticeship most other forms of training in general industry appear to be carried on in a very casual and informal fashion. In most instances this would appear to be all that is called for. Such training is largely confined to the acquisition of the specialized skills which are often required of semi-skilled operatives. For this purpose anything more than informal on-the-job training would appear to be unnecessary.

Outside of the traditional fields of blue collar work, however, this is less likely to be the case. For many service and commercial occupations more training of a pre-employment nature may have to be carried on by employers if our high schools are to avoid over-specialization at too early an age. While there are no doubt exceptions to the general rule, it is our view that industry would be very short-sighted to insist on a finished product from the high schools. We realize that this is not the case today. We venture to suggest, however, that it is likely to become increasingly unrealistic to expect fully trained high-school products in the future. It is our view that it will be in industry's own interest to carry a greater share of specialized training than it has heretofore shouldered. This would permit the secondary schools to provide the broadly based type of vocational training which we feel is going to become increasingly essential to prepare people for the periodic retraining they may have to undergo during their working lives. Such retraining is probably unavoidable and unless industry is prepared to do more of the initial training of new entrants into its work force, it will so constrain the schools as to complicate the periodic retraining which industry itself is likely to have to undertake in the future.

We do not see how industry can be easily induced or compelled to bear a greater share of the overall responsibility for specialized vocational preparation. We hope that its own self-interest will eventually dictate an appropriate course of action in this regard. We therefore urge industry to continually reassess its position in this matter. We feel that if it does so, it will soon adopt the practices of those firms which are already doing a great deal in this area.

---

[1] Not all other forms of training in general industry are dealt with in this section. Supervisory development and measures designed to upgrade workers who otherwise would be displaced from their jobs are covered in later parts of the Report.

SPECIAL PROGRAMS FOR TRAINING OR RETRAINING PARTICULAR CATEGORIES OF ADULT WORKERS

Under this heading we would like to discuss the need for a variety of programs designed to improve the skills of our non-school age adult population. Some of these programs may be readily operated in conjunction with the programs and facilities discussed earlier in this Report. Others will require the addition of special new programs or facilities. In either event the needs are so distinct from those already described that separate attention should be devoted to them.

(i) Before examining individual programs at the adult level, we would like to emphasize our view that adult education and training is bound to become increasingly important in the years ahead. In this connection we would hazard the guess that before very long our adult education and training programs will be so vast and complex as to command as much attention as our normal day-school operations. For this reason we strongly endorse the idea of employing full-time coordinators of adult education wherever it is economically feasible to do so.

(ii) We also would like to commend the recent addition of special Adult Education Centres in both Cornwall and Toronto. While we recognize the need to utilize existing physical facilities and to avoid unnecessary duplication, we also recognize that there are many advantages to having at least one separate and distinct adult education centre in every large city.

We would now like to turn to a review of our specific needs at the adult level.

Salvaging Drop-outs and Enhancing Their Employability

We have already had a great deal to say about the problem of drop-outs. Although we anticipate that the introduction of the Robarts Plan will reduce the present proportions of this problem, we realize that it will not eliminate it altogether. For this reason we urge that the need for remedial efforts designed to deal with the difficulties likely to confront such individuals be not neglected.

Since those who drop out of school almost never apply for public assistance to enable them to acquire training in a specific skill or occupation unless they are unemployed, they can usually be dealt with under Program 5 (Training of the Unemployed) of the Federal-Provincial Vocational Training Agreement. Since this program is discussed at some length in the next section of this Report, there is no need to duplicate that discussion here. We would like to make one or two points, however, in connection with the particular problems posed by school drop-outs.

(i) In the first place, to avoid drop-outs who leave secondary school in order to qualify for assisted training under Program 5, we recommend the continuation and general adoption of the policy implemented by the Provincial Institute of Trades whereby no drop-out is accepted into a Program 5 course until at least six months after he leaves school. We wholeheartedly endorse the thinking behind this policy.

(ii) Secondly, we would like to record a reservation as to whether a straight-forward program designed to enhance the employability of drop-outs is likely to prove sufficient in times of unduly heavy unemployment. We have already shown that education and training do not provide the key to full employment. Added to this is the fact that unemployment consistently bears much more heavily on our young people than it does on the work force as a whole. This means that a number of our young people may easily find themselves unemployed despite the partial acquisition of a particular skill.[1] Since this is a trying period in any person's development, we question the wisdom of permitting these people to remain unemployed for any length of time.

To prevent the deterioration in skill and morale which can readily result from such an experience, we suggest that consideration be given to the establishment of youth camps which would combine both work experience and further education and training. If structured along the lines of the old Youth Conservation Corps in the United States during the 1930's, such a medium could provide a constructive alternative to a period of enforced idleness. It would provide an excellent outlet for the energies of such persons and could fill a needed gap in the vital years of their development.

---

[1] If there is a great deal of general unemployment even young people who are fully trained may not be able to find employment.

The Ontario Federation of Labour made a somewhat similar suggestion (Proceedings, pp. 562-3):

> We urge that consideration be given to setting up "work schools" for young men and young women where they can go through a co-ordinated and co-related program: "Work, Earn and Learn". Such a program should be most appropriate for and appeal to our young people who have completed or dropped out of their formal courses but who have been unable to establish themselves in permanent employment. . . .
>
> Part of each day would be given to formal and consistent educational programs, and part to productive employment. The young people would be paid both on the basis of their academic achievement and their work assignments. All work assignments at the school, whether they be maintenance, cooking, dishwashing or driving trucks, could be made part of the learning process and integrated into the educational program. When a young person left such a school after a term or season, he would be better educated, have some work experience to stand in good stead with a future employer, and also have some money in his pocket.

Training Unemployed Workers Who Have Obsolete Skills or Who Are Relatively Unskilled

No more telling problem confronts us today in the field of manpower development than that of training those of our unemployed workers who lack any marketable skill or occupation. The problem is greatly aggravated by the low level of academic proficiency which has been characteristic of many of our unemployed workers over the past few years. In the face of rising skill requirements on the demand side of the labour market, these people have been at a particular disadvantage during recent periods of heavy unemployment. The position of such individuals was aptly described by a representative of the International Correspondence Schools (Proceedings, pp. 366-7):

> It is becoming more widely recognized that a significant number of Ontario's unemployed people are technically "unemployable". Because they lack skills, possess obsolete or no longer wanted skills, or in some cases lack the educational qualifications now required for technical training, there is apparently scant prospect of their return to the work force. They are largely "unemployable" and in their present lack and need of training can only be regarded as a welfare charge against the state—which will, under present circumstances, become more burdensome, more undesirable and more futilely wasteful of people and their potential as time goes on.

To help correct this situation Program 5 (Training of the Unemployed) was included as one of the programs under the Federal-Provincial Technical and Vocational Training Agreement Act. Although Ontario was somewhat slow in taking advantage of this portion of the agreement, it attained the necessary number of man-days in the first partial years of operation and now is fully committed to a comprehensive program in this area. During the current year (April 1, 1962 to March 31, 1963) it is estimated that at least 800,000 man-days will be devoted to the training of unemployed workers in this Province. By the end of November 500,387 man-days had already been expended. For a program which is only in its second year of full-time operation, this is a remarkable achievement.

(i) A significant issue in the minds of the members of the Committee has been the question of compulsion in relation to this scheme. At the present time, the unemployed worker who possesses an obsolete skill or no skill at all is under no compulsion to take training even if he is collecting unemployment insurance. Whether or not there should be an element of compulsion is debatable. The case for some sort of compulsion has been succinctly put by Bascom St. John:

> Undoubtedly the time will come when compulsory education, now accepted for children and youth, will have to be broadened to include other classes of people. No more harm would be done to civil liberty by requiring adults to learn new occupations than is now done by forcing children to attend school. In both cases, it has to be agreed that ignorance is not a basic right of the individual.[1]

There is no doubt that there is a great deal of appeal in this argument. At the present time, however, this Committee does not feel we should go quite this far. On the practical side there is the obvious problem of motivation. If the worker has to be compelled to undergo training it is questionable whether he will get very much out of it. Beyond this there are the deeper philosophic dimensions of the problem. It is one thing to force a child or juvenile to go to school; it is another to compel an adult to undergo retraining.

(ii) Instead of introducing compulsion we would suggest that greater financial assistance be given to those unemployed workers who

---

[1] Bascom St. John, "Should Jobless Be Forced to Learn New Occupations", *The Globe & Mail*, October 5, 1962.

are willing to undergo training. It is our impression that the present margin between unemployment insurance and the subsistence payments which a worker is eligible to receive under Program 5 is too narrow. We would recommend that this differential be widened so as to make it more attractive to undergo training.

The present allowances are so low that many workers prefer to stay on unemployment insurance in the hope of finding employment rather than commit themselves to any sort of prolonged training program. In this connection the Committee has been very impressed by the fact that most West European countries appear to provide much more generous allowances, relative to their normal pay, to workers who are undergoing training. As much as anything else this probably accounts for the higher percentage of their unemployed workers who appear to respond to these programs.

(iii) Related to the previous point is the fact that unemployed workers who are eligible for unemployment insurance use up their unemployment insurance credits during their training period even though they receive no higher allowances than those who are not eligible for unemployment benefits. We suggest that this is a grave inequity and that the Province of Ontario should make representation to the Federal Government to rectify the situation. The unemployed worker's equity in the unemployment insurance fund should be protected while he is undergoing training. Either that or he should receive a higher training allowance than those who are not eligible for or have exhausted their unemployment benefits.

(iv) Despite the attention which we have devoted to monetary considerations, it is to be emphasized that adequate financial inducement is only part of the answer. How complicated the question of motivation for unemployed workers can be is suggested by the testimony of the Social Planning Council of Metropolitan Toronto (Proceedings, p. 1212):

> Learning cannot be forced and it is doubtful if punitive approaches to training would accomplish hoped for objectives. Incentives must replace coercion. Job opportunities must await graduates, and trainees must find it economically possible to enroll and remain in training while continuing to meet ongoing financial obligations as adults.

> Generally, community attitudes do not help as adult education is not commonly accepted in our society in the same way as is universal public education for children. An individual who feels secure in a job may see no need for upgrading. The unemployed man is confronted with feelings of failure, inadequacy and depression often leading to increasing deterioration to the point where any desire for improvement training or even work itself can be lost.
>
> Training programs then must recognize the factors of motivation and the human element involved. The need for special services and approaches in providing training must be accepted if the objective of such training programs is to be fully achieved.

We urge that all those who are involved in our training programs for unemployed workers become more familiar with these considerations and make due allowance for them.

(v) As suggested previously, one of the most serious challenges we face in the field of training the unemployed pertains to the need to upgrade them to the point where they can absorb any kind of advanced training. For this purpose, a course entitled Basic Training for Skill Development has been introduced under Program 5. We commend the Federal Government for interpreting the legislation to be flexible enough to allow for such a course and urge that continued use be made of it. If this type of course is kept as practical as possible and is taught in conjunction with related shopwork, it will serve an invaluable purpose.

(vi) In connection with the latter point we would like to emphasize the need for special techniques in teaching adult workers. Although much has already been done to develop such techniques this is a subject which is bound to require increasing attention in the years ahead. An indication of the degree of rethinking which may have to be done in this area is provided in *A Brief Submitted by a Citizens' Committee Concerned with the Educational Upgrading of Early School Leavers* which was prepared for the Anglican Information Centre in Toronto in December 1961. As quoted in the presentation of the Social Planning Council of Metropolitan Toronto to this Committee (Proceedings, pp. 1205-7), the most pertinent findings of this group were as follows:

> Experience in our projects so far has shown that content of courses can make a great difference in motivating adult students. It would seem, then, advisable to re-write academic courses in terms of the

content of the trades-training which they are intended to precede, in order that trainees may see the utility and purpose of the work demanded of them. Further, experience shows that the two skills most required in trade courses are reading and arithmetic, and that the skills of self-expression are less essential.

It has been found that use of the grade system for adults causes them to see themselves in an unfavourable and discouraging light by comparison with their own children. When this happens they tend to become discouraged from attending classes. The grade school system has been the scene of the first of their failures, and in most cases the failures which have set the stage for a succession of failures. To expect them to return to this scene with any confidence is to expect more than most of us, who have not known anything like the same degree of defeat, could manage. Moreover, the realization of the parents' relatively low level of achievement in academic subjects seems to obviate for their children the necessity to persevere in the more demanding grades and to encourage them to drop out of school before attaining the maximum of which they are capable. A different method of evaluating adult achievement could help to overcome both these problems.

(vii) Our final observation pertains to the initiation of Program 5 courses. At the present time this is left up to local municipalities. It may well be that in the future consideration will have to be given to the Provincial Department of Education playing a greater role in these matters. For the present, however, we would not deem this wise. Only recently have many communities become aware of Program 5. More and more of them are now taking advantage of it.

Upgrading of Employed Persons Who Otherwise Would be Displaced from Their Jobs

A challenge of growing significance relates to the problem of employed workers who are gradually made obsolete by technological change or other developments. In many cases such individuals could probably hold on to their existing jobs or transfer to other jobs if they could be provided with the requisite skill. Where this is possible it stands to reason that it would be far more economical to upgrade workers in order to maintain them in their current employment rather than to wait for them to be displaced and then retrain them for some other line of activity.

That this is possible has been shown in many instances. Both voluntarily and as a result of contract obligations, numerous employers have upgraded many thousands of workers to equip them for more demanding jobs. Very often this is done on the job or through the medium of evening programs and thus costs very little. In other cases it may require the employer to remove workers altogether from the job in order to give them more intensive training. Where this is necessary the costs can soon become prohibitive. It is at this point that government assistance may be required.

We strongly endorse the idea of such assistance and urge that consideration be given to it under Program 4 of the Federal-Provincial Agreement. We would hope that Program 4 would be interpreted in as liberal a fashion as Program 5 so that basic training for skill development could be included as a major facet of the type of upgrading discussed in this section.

Facilitating the Integration of Immigrants into Constructive Employment

The manpower training needs of many recent arrivals in this country are very great indeed. During the past few years a high percentage of immigrants coming to Canada have lacked a readily marketable skill or occupation. In addition to this many have had very little academic education beyond the equivalent of our senior public school grades. When combined with their lack of fluency in the English language, these handicaps have placed many immigrants at a serious disadvantage in the labour market.

While it is true that these deficiencies—except the language barrier—are no different than those afflicting numerous native-born Canadians, the special problems confronting many immigrants are sufficiently complex to merit separate consideration. Even though the problems of the two groups are somewhat comparable, the unskilled immigrant often faces unique difficulties which are not experienced by the unskilled worker who has been born and bred in Canada. Although most of these unique difficulties stem from the language problem, there are also other factors at work.

Dealing first with the question of lack of fluency in the English language the Committee has deliberately avoided the pitfall of considering this need in the context of over-all immigrant policy. We have thus avoided the issue as to whether all immigrants should be expected or required to learn English when they come to English-speaking parts of Canada. Instead we have concentrated on the language needs of immigrants strictly in terms of the employment requirements they are likely to run into. With this in mind, it is our view that the teaching of English to unemployed immigrants should be confined to condensed courses which stress the indispensable elements of the language. The emphasis should be placed on the bare essentials likely to be required of them on the job for which they have or are being prepared. For those who wish to demand much more English of immigrants other means must be sought. Where upgrading or training of immigrants is involved, unduly demanding language requirements should not be permitted to subvert the basic purpose of equipping these people with marketable talents as expeditiously as possible. In so far as it is possible to do so the teaching of English in these cases should be confined to practical instruction in the trade or industrial use of the language.

Where extended instruction in English is required it should be combined with training in a trade or occupation. Proper motivation would appear to make this mandatory. Because of this the immigrant may acquire a solid grounding in a trade or occupation before he actually enters it. Where apprenticeship is involved appropriate credit should be allowed for the extended practical training which the immigrant has received in the course of picking up a sufficient knowledge of English.

Related to the previous point is the need to provide bilingual instruction in trade and related subjects wherever language presents a serious problem. It is senseless to try to impart a great deal of knowledge to people in a short period of time in a language which is still somewhat foreign to them. It is obvious, however, that bilingual instruction can only be offered where there is a sufficient number of immigrants to make it economical.

It likewise follows that wherever examinations and tests are involved, immigrants who lack fluency in English should either be permitted to answer questions in their native language or be permitted the use of an interpreter. We commend the Apprenticeship Branch for employing just such a practice in the case of non-Egnlish speaking immigrants who are attempting to qualify for journeyman standing.

In so far as the teaching of English itself is concerned we are much more reticent about recommending bilingual instruction. Although the instructors employed for such purposes should be conversant in the native language(s) of their students, we would deem it a mistake to overemphasize the use of bilingual instruction in this regard. In the teaching of foreign languages, we have been led to believe that the most effective means is to expose people to a heavy and persistent dose of the new language with little or no instruction in their native tongue.

Another matter which requires some attention relates to the question of the amount of credit which immigrants should be given for the academic education they have acquired before coming to Canada. This is often a most vexing problem. It seems most unfair to think that an immigrant may be prevented from directly pursuing a particular career because he cannot prove the equivalency of a specific grade level in this country. We can only suggest that everything possible should be done to break down such obstacles without, at the same time, sacrificing the standards of proficiency which are prevalent in the affected trades or occupations. Where some sort of graded certification is put into effect this can probably be much more readily accomplished. We would caution, however, that we cannot afford to be too lenient with immigrants with regard to academic qualifications without discriminating against native-born Canadians and jeopardizing the very standards which we are trying to build up.

Beyond these general questions our first set of remarks pertains to immigrants who arrive here fully or partially trained in a particular trade or occupation. With regard to those in the former category it may seem as though there should be no real problem. Unfortunately this is not always the case. In the first place immigrants may arrive here with a complete training in a trade or occupation as it is practiced in their native land, but find that there are subtle or none-too-subtle differences between the training which they have received and that which is provided for those entering similar trades or occupations in Canada. Secondly, they may have a serious language problem to overcome. In either or both of these instances it would be uneconomic and unfair to waste the potentially valuable talents of such individuals in their chosen trades or occupations.

Where lack of familiarity with the peculiar facets of a trade or occupation as practiced in Canada is the only problem it can be readily overcome. All that is required in these cases is a series of familiarization classes or a specially designed and greatly abbreviated apprenticeship program. Where language also presents some difficulty such training would have to be combined with instruction in the English language.

Similar although more lengthy programs would likewise be required for those who arrive with only partial training in a particular trade or occupation. Where apprenticeship is the accepted medium of training it would largely be a problem of determining how much credit should be given such individuals. Otherwise it would be a matter of providing specific types of classroom instruction and/or on-the-job training to accomplish the desired objective.

Where immigrants arrive here with little or no education and training—academic or otherwise—as well as with serious language problems, it is unrealistic to conceive of preparing them for skilled trades or occupations. Instead the emphasis in these cases will have to be placed on the acquisition of less demanding skills. Training for many service occupations might prove suitable in this regard. Beyond this such individuals should probably be left to the same resources as other Canadians.

This brings us to our final point with respect to the education and training of immigrants. While the major focus must be upon unemployed immigrants, everything possible should be done to provide for the needs of employed immigrants as well. Evening programs provide an excellent medium for this purpose. If through part-time programs we can upgrade the skills of such people and improve their fluency in the English language we are likely to reduce the dimensions of our future problems in this area. Even more farsighted would be a policy designed to equip immigrants for various types of employment immediately upon their arrival in Canada. Instead of waiting for them to become unemployed, before we do something about their plight, it would seem far more sensible to try to improve the marketability of their skills prior to their actually entering the labour market.

By way of summarizing our views with respect to the education and training of immigrants, we would like to put forward the following proposals:

(i) Where lack of fluency in the English language is a problem, emphasis should be placed upon the use of condensed courses which concentrate on the fundamentals of the language and which stress the acquisition of practical work-oriented English. This applies particularly where the English is taught as part of our general program for training the unemployed. Further acquaintance with the English language should be left to part-time courses.

(ii) Whenever sufficient numbers are involved, immigrants who lack fluency in the English language should be taught trade and related subjects by bilingual instructors.

(iii) Likewise, wherever examinations and tests are involved, immigrants who lack fluency in English should either be permitted to answer questions in their native language or be permitted the use of an interpreter.

(iv) Where immigrants are concerned, particular care must be taken to ensure that grade or equivalency qualifications for specific trades and occupations are not administered unfairly.

(v) Under Program 5 special care will have to be taken in designing courses to suit the needs of unemployed immigrants. Where sufficient numbers respond to such courses, they should be so structured and sub-divided as to meet the diverse needs of the various categories of immigrants outlined above.

(vi) Although Program 5 offers the most effective medium through which immigrants can be made more readily employable, other possibilities should not be neglected. Aside from upgrading the skills of those already employed, some consideration should also be given to the establishment of special full-time programs designed to better prepare the immigrant for work immediately upon his arrival in Canada.

Rehabilitating Inmates of Penal Institutions

In the course of its investigations the Committee has been most impressed by the work which is being done in our penal institutions to rehabilitate inmates by providing them with a marketable skill or occupation. We recognize these programs as another important element in our overall education and training system. We urge that they be continued and that everything possible be done to integrate their planning with related developments in education and training in the Province as a whole. With this in mind we urge that the Department of Education play a greater role in the development and operation of these programs. While it would not be wise to turn over complete responsibility for education and training in our penal institutions to the Department of Education, it does seem desirable that it be given as great a role as possible. This would ensure that the rehabilitation programs in our penal institutions meet the necessary standards and would further ensure that those who successfully complete such programs receive proper recognition for their accomplishment.

Rehabilitating Disabled and Handicapped Persons

Much of what we have said in connection with rehabilitation work in our penal institutions is equally applicable to the work which is being done to rehabilitate disabled and handicapped persons. Between the Workmen's Compensation Board and the many private bodies which are active in this type of work (such as the Canadian National Institute for the Blind and the Canadian Association for Retarded Children), an excellent foundation has been laid for any additional work which may be required in these areas.

In all of these fields we strongly support the policy of reducing our institutionalized and dependent population by providing them with some degree of employability. Not only does this reduce the cost to the public of maintaining these people but it contributes greatly to their own well being by making their lives more meaningful and self-sufficient.

Where private means are not sufficient and public facilities are not now available, primary consideration should be given to the subsidization of existing private groups who are already active in the field. As we become more aware of the dimensions of the problems we face in these areas, we are going to have to face the fact that such subsidies may have to be increased substantially. At a certain point in time it may then become necessary to transfer the entire responsibility for certain types of rehabilitation work to the public domain, just as we have done in the case of workmen's compensation in this Province.

One matter which even now appears to require that degree of public participation, pertains to the question of sheltered workshops and sheltered hostels. Many disabled or handicapped workers are not able to hold down a regular job but are capable of doing a few hours of specially regulated work per day. To deny them this opportunity is both wasteful and cruel. Often the only way to provide them with such an outlet is through the medium of sheltered workshops. These can never be completely self-sustaining entities but they can be a more economical device for occupying the time of handicapped persons than any other form of specialized institutional treatment. Through a sheltered workshop program, disabled and handicapped workers who otherwise would have to be permanently institutionalized may be enabled to live at home and avoid a regimented existence.

For many of these individuals, however, home does not offer a meaningful alternative. Either they are homeless or the home does not afford some of the conditions which are essential to their balance and equilibrium. Likewise, there may be others who can survive in certain types of regular employment but who also require a special kind of leisure time atmosphere. For all of these individuals the concept of a sheltered hostel may offer the only alternative to complete institutionalization. As in the case of the sheltered workshop, the advantages to all concerned are considerable.

We would thus recommend that consideration be given to the establishment of government-operated sheltered workshops and hostels or to the subsidization of private groups (as in the case of the Canadian National Institute for the Blind) who are willing to operate one or other, or both, of such undertakings.

To conclude our comments with regard to the training of handicapped and disabled persons, we would like to endorse the following assessment by the Social Planning Council of Metropolitan Toronto of the existing situation and of our future needs in these areas (Proceedings, p. 1239):

> Existing programs for the handicapped related to manpower training under both public and voluntary auspices, are receiving increasing emphasis. Examples include the provincial rehabilitation services, Workmen's Compensation Board, and various voluntary workshops and vocational services. Facilities and staffs are limited, however, and continued emphasis must be placed on strengthening services, increasing qualified staffs, and in every way possible giving support to the further development of both Government and voluntary programs.

THE ROLE OF PRIVATE TRADE SCHOOLS AND CORRESPONDENCE SCHOOLS

Also worthy of note as part of our overall program for training and developing manpower in Ontario is the role played by private trade schools (including commercial and business schools) and correspondence schools. In a number of cases the courses offered through these media have helped to fill serious gaps in our general education and training system. As a result they have sometimes set an example for later public ventures in the same fields.

Some of the courses offered by the various types of private schools have been of a very high order. Students have received all that they could have asked for and have been satisfactorily placed upon graduation.

Unfortunately the record of the legitimate private schools has sometimes been marred by the activities of less reputable entrepreneurs. Private trade schools and correspondence schools which operate solely with a view to making a profit normally do not survive for a long period of time. In the meantime, however, much damage will have been done to those who have enrolled in such schools. For this reason it is our firm conviction that all private trade schools and correspondence schools should be regulated much more rigorously than is the case at present. Every effort should be made to keep the fly-by-night charlatans out of the field. There must be constant vigilance and repeated inspections by competent persons familiar with the training in question in order to ensure that schools are offering nothing less than they purport to offer.

Where a particular trade or occupation appears to be especially susceptible to infiltration by illegitimate private schools, consideration should be given to exclusive public sponsorship of the training in question. Because we believe that there is an appropriate role for legitimate private schools, however, we do not believe that such institutions as a group should be deliberately prohibited or regulated out of existence. All we should aim for is sufficiently rigorous regulation to eliminate shady operations before they have a chance either to harm the public or to detract from the reputation of the legitimate private schools.

SUPERVISORY TRAINING AND MANAGEMENT DEVELOPMENT

One of our economy's most pressing needs is for competent personnel at all levels in our managerial hierarchy. In the past it has not been thought necessary to place a great deal of emphasis on formal training in the filling of such positions. Since the war this has rapidly given way to an ever-increasing interest in formal methods for developing managerial talents. Today there is less and less opportunity to rise through "the school of hard knocks" and more and more demand for specially trained individuals. Although there are advantages to both approaches, this Committee firmly believes that managers of the future will require considerably more technical know-how and that this will inevitably lead to a greater emphasis on formal training.

Despite the importance which we attach to the development of top-rate managerial talent we are reluctant to suggest that the government move into this area on a wholesale basis. Instead it is our view that this should remain primarily the responsibility of industry itself. This reflects our belief that training in particular managerial skills can probably best be acquired by a combination of on-the-job experience and classroom instruction. If we are correct in this assessment, then the government should concentrate its efforts on the development of a general education system which is capable of turning out high-quality students who can readily respond to these types of programs.

At the same time, however, we do not wish to minimize the more specific roles which the government can play in this field. By building up the Business and Commerce stream of the high school vocational program and by promoting more advanced work in the managerial sciences at the technical institute and university levels, the government can do a great deal to develop a sound foundation of business education upon which various firms and industries can fashion programs geared to their own particular needs. Moreover, by offering special extension courses in business subjects, our schools can supplement industry's on-the-job training programs. At more advanced levels the universities should be encouraged and assisted to continue and expand their special programs for middle-line and senior executives.

The government may have to go somewhat farther to provide for the needs of businessmen and first-line supervisors in small and medium size firms. Before directly sponsoring courses in these areas, however, the government should give every consideration to the use and extension of existing private programs. Only when all other possibilities are exhausted (i.e. as in the case of small businessmen in small towns) should the government operate its own special programs. We note with interest that this is exactly what the Management Training Division of the Small Business Administration Section of the Department of Trade and Commerce in Ottawa is planning to do. Should the Province of Ontario decide to do anything in this area care will have to be taken to ensure that there is not unnecessary duplication. We would also venture to suggest that in so far as the government—either federal or provincial—does move into this area, the various programs offered should be administered and co-ordinated by the Provincial Department of Education. Such programs should be viewed as part of our overall education and training system and should be properly integrated into that system.

PART IV

RELATED COMMENTS AND RECOMMENDATIONS

RESEARCH — A NEGLECTED BUT VITAL NEED

THE development of an educational and training system which is geared to the unfolding needs of a changing labour force can be no more than wishful thinking unless a continuing program of research is carried on. Such a program must be designed to identify the nature of our future manpower needs, to throw light on the consequences of these needs for education and training policies, and to assess the effectiveness of various education and training activities.

Nothing has disturbed this Committee more than the paucity of research which has so far been undertaken in this country in each of these areas. Not only do we lack sufficient information on the past and present composition of the labour force, and on the future outlook in this regard, but we also have very little knowledge about the effectiveness of our existing educational and training programs.

The deficient state of our information in these and in other respects must quickly be overcome if we are to have any hope of developing and maintaining sound programs to prepare our labour force for the challenges of the future.

Forecasting Changes in the Nature and Composition of the Labour Force

A paramount question which every government should be asking itself and trying to find an answer to on a systematic and continuing basis, is "what are the current and future needs of the economy for trained manpower?" Manpower shortage and outlook information is required, in occupational and geographical detail where feasible, because important decisions about education and training should only be taken in the light of such information and related research findings.

There is considerably more information available in this country with respect to what has happened, is happening, and will likely happen to the occupational composition of the labour force than is generally realized. Better means of making this information available to those who need it is an absolute must. Beyond this, however, there will still remain the need to greatly extend and improve upon the information which now can be readily produced. There is a need both for more quantitative and for more qualitative information, especially with regard to the future outlook.

What we have now is a limited range of broad projections. On the quantitative side, for example, a great deal of effort has been made to predict the number of new entrants into the labour force in the next few years. Similarly, some general predictions have been made with regard to the probable occupational composition of labour demand in the forseeable future. Very little has been done, however, to link these two types of studies together. While we now have a rough idea how many new workers will be entering the labour market and what kind of jobs will be available for them, we have not approached these matters in as logical and definitive a fashion as we should have. As adequate as our overall occupational forecasts may be for postulating general trends in the skill composition of the labour force, they are somewhat wanting in terms of more specific developments. Equally serious is our lack of more detailed knowledge on the supply side of the market. Although projections have been made as to what is likely to happen to our total labour supply almost nothing is available on the probable qualifications of future entrants into the labour force.

The inadequate state of our knowledge in these respects is most unfortunate. As a Committee we have felt the need for more definitive information about these matters over and over again. We know that those who have had to make vital decisions with regard to the allocation of our resources in the field of education and training have felt this need much more so than ourselves. We commend them for having the courage to make the decisions which they have had to make in the absence of adequate information. We wonder, however, how long they can go on doing this before an unwitting but drastic misallocation of resources occurs.

Since our entire system of education and training must of necessity be based on anticipated manpower needs, it stands to reason that we must make a much greater effort to project our future requirements. Unless we do something to correct this situation immediately all of the recommendations which we have advanced will be worth little more than the paper they are written on. Without a system of continuing forecasting there is no possible way in which we can hope to keep our education and training system as fully up-to-date and effective as possible.

We note with interest that *The Report of the Special Committee of the Senate on Manpower and Employment* showed equal concern about the crucial role to be played by forecasting:[1]

> More specifically, steps should be taken immediately to initiate a continuous and comprehensive program designed to provide periodic analyses and forecasts of the size and composition of the labour force and the demand for workers in different industries, areas, occupations, and with different skills. The results of these studies should be given wide publicity. It is not sufficient that the government of the day be correctly informed on these matters, although it goes without saying that this is of fundamental importance. The public must also be informed. Our teachers, educational administrators, employers, labour unions, and others must be fully acquainted with the changes that are taking place. Up to the present the situation has not been satisfactory in this regard. A program such as this is an urgent requirement if we are to avoid the danger of training today's youth for yesterday's jobs.

In urging that more forecasting be undertaken in this country, we wish to make it clear that we recognize that there are limitations to what can be done in this regard. We realize for example, that it is completely unrealistic to expect to be able to predict exactly what will happen to the demand for a particular occupation over some specified future period. This would require a degree of precision

---

[1] The Senate of Canada, *The Report of the Special Committee of the Senate on Manpower and Employment*, op. cit., p. 7.

which is beyond the realm of possibility and for that reason could be most deceptive. One of the basic objectives of manpower forecasting, therefore, should be the development of criteria which can be used for deciding when occupational forecasts are so unreliable as to be potentially and dangerously misleading.

Even in attempting to ascertain less specific information we do not wish to minimize the difficulties which are likely to be involved. With the number of variables which have to be taken into consideration there are bound to be errors and mistakes. We would submit, however, that on balance it is likely to be far less costly in the long run to plan on the basis of forecasts, even allowing for a fairly significant margin of error, than to proceed with little or no forecasting at all. A well-developed forecast would surely provide a far more assuring basis for planning than a haphazard estimate or even an educated guess.

In the long run we would suggest that two distinctive types of forecasts should be developed. One should cover a more distant time span, say the outlook between five and ten years ahead, and the other should concentrate on the more immediate future. In each case it would not be sufficient to attempt to forecast manpower requirements simply on a mechanistic basis. It is important that the assumptions which underlie any forecasts (i.e. as to overall growth rates, anticipated technological changes, and so on) should rest on a more solid basis of research than is the case at present. To make the kinds of manpower forecasts needed to assist in the formulation and implementation of educational and training programs, intensive analyses of the changing industrial structure of the economy is necessary. This in turn will require a careful discernment and assessment of the causes of industrial change.

It would obviously be far more difficult to pin down these factors for the longer range forecast than it would be for the more immediate one. We would not expect, therefore, as precise information from the former. Instead we would look for general trends which might be of particular interest to those structuring the broad vocational programs which we have already suggested will become increasingly necessary at the high school level.

We would expect that the more immediate forecast would provide us with more precise information as to the general outlook for specific trades and occupations in the near future. This is the kind of information which should be channeled to those working on specialized training.

A study of past and present occupational trends would be of great value to those engaged in the task of short term forecasting. Much use can be made of such data in themselves, since they provide a good indication of current needs, persistent shortages, and expanding or declining occupations. There are numerous sources of data which can be used for this purpose. Much information is already in the hands of such federal agencies as the National Employment Service, the Dominion Bureau of Statistics and the Department of Labour.

With regard to the amount of information which might be made available through the National Employment Service, it is our view that this agency should be much more conversant with existing vacancies in the labour market than it has been to date. At the present time many employers do not avail themselves of the services provided by N.E.S. and do not list their openings with it unless they are desperate. To provide us with a continuing inventory of present needs, it is our view that N.E.S. should make use of the power it now has to require all employers to list their vacancies with it on a monthly basis. To avoid saddling employers with an unduly heavy reporting burden this requirement could be substituted for the present data which employers submit on a monthly basis with respect to hirings and separations. We would suggest that the Province make appropriate representations to the federal authorities in this regard. In doing so they should be careful to point out that the obligation to report vacancies would in no way compel the employer to utilize the good offices of the N.E.S. He would still be free to hire whomever he pleased.

As a further extension of the latter suggestion we would also recommend that much more use be made of properly designed surveys to determine the needs which employers anticipate in the future. While we recognize the defects inherent in such surveys, it is our belief that with careful nurturing they could provide an excellent supplement to more theoretical forecasting techniques.

To ensure the effective utilization of such surveys, major reliance should be placed on questionnaires directed to firms which have shown sufficient interest in such a program to participate in its development and improvement.

Developing and Improving Our Educational and Training Methods

Just as vital as the need for the various types of forecasts outlined in the previous section is the need to develop appropriate educational and training policies to meet the requirements suggested by the various forecasts. This will require considerable research into a variety of areas. With regard to forecasts on the demand side of the labour market, for example, care will have to be taken to ensure that the forecast determines what is likely to happen to the skill content of particular jobs as well as to the number of such jobs which are likely to be available. There will thus be the need to avoid the use of superficial job titles which denote little or nothing about the actual requirements of the job. Just as important as the foregoing will be the need for research to explore how the various skills called for in different occupations can best be imparted.

Equally important is the matter of improving teaching and training techniques. There is an urgent need, for example, for the development of more effective methods for adult training. How can adults be most effectively instructed in basic subject matter areas, such as mathematics and science? How can classroom instruction and on-the-job experience be most effectively integrated in the training of adults? What is the role of programmed learning in the teaching of adults? These are but a few of the questions which require attention. A good deal of thought is being given to adult training techniques in Western Europe and elsewhere, and by such organizations as the I.L.O. and the O.E.C.D., and the results of such efforts can serve as a basis for similar activity in Canada.

Assessing the Record

To assist in each of the former areas, we are going to have to initiate a continuing audit of our educational and training system in relation to the demands made upon it. Among other things this will have to entail an on-going study of the factors which lead students to drop out of school and an assessment of what happens to those who successfully complete various educational programs. The latter would almost certainly have to include a detailed analysis of how people actually acquire the skills which eventually provide them with a livelihood.

There is also a need to evaluate the role of the labour market as an allocator of manpower. It is vital to know how the labour market is operating, if only to gain an understanding of how effective it can be in meeting our needs for various types of skilled labour. It may well be that when a shortage of manpower appears in certain occupations it is not always necessary to think in terms of special training programs. In some cases it might be better to facilitate the operation of the labour market so that it can more effectively serve to re-allocate or substitute manpower already available to meet the new need.

Responsibility for Research

We cannot afford to neglect the many types of research which are called for in this section of the Report simply because of divisions of opinion over who should be responsible for it. Research in many of the areas discussed has already been initiated and carried forward for some years by the Federal Government, and particularly by the Department of Labour. A range of useful studies has been, and is being, conducted under the Department of Labour's Skilled Manpower Training Research Program and other programs in such areas as technological change, occupational trends and developments, vocational training needs both in schools and in industry, and the development of techniques for long-range manpower forecasting. The burden of manpower research should be shared, however, by other agencies as well. Not only is there room for, but it is imperative that, research activities of the type outlined should be carried out to a much greater extent than in the past by the Provincial Government. Even if the Federal Government greatly steps up its efforts in these fields—as it must—Ontario will still have to supplement these efforts in terms of its own needs. What is really required is a co-operative approach on the part of the two levels of government, including where practical the conducting of research on a joint basis.

This sort of co-operation is also required on the part of the various departments within the Provincial Government which have a legitimate interest in the field of manpower research. How the three departments involved — Labour, Education, and Economics and Development—decide to divide up their responsibilities in this area is not of fundamental importance. What is more essential is the need for them to sit down together at the operating level, agree on what information they should develop, and get on with it.

Aside from the matter of forecasting, the bulk of the responsibility would seem to lie with the Department of Education. Once all of the available data has been brought together it will be up to the Department to draw from it the appropriate implications. It will likewise be up to the Department to ensure that the most effective means are being employed to prepare the labour force for the job requirements of the future. To provide for a continuing assessment of the performance of our educational and training system in relation to those requirements, much more research will have to be carried on by the Department. It is going to have to become far more research-oriented than it has ever been in the past.

Finally, it must be recognized that if effective research is to be carried out in the manpower field—regardless of who is responsible for it—adequate staff and financial resources must be provided. Until a competent staff can be brought together at the governmental level and probably even after that, ample use should be made of the research talents of outside experts. The growing magnitude of our investment in education and training, and the benefits to be gained from such research in terms of the better utilization and allocation of our human resources, make it essential that we spend whatever is necessary to get experts to work on these matters as soon as possible.

VOCATIONAL GUIDANCE

Just as significant as continuing research to the effective implementation of an overall educational and training system is the provision of adequate vocational guidance. With the world of work changing ever more rapidly and becoming increasingly complex, we cannot afford to neglect the critical role of career planning. Without it we cannot hope to match the varying interests, aptitudes and abilities of the members of our work force with the ever-widening and constantly changing variety of our labour requirements.

The importance of vocational guidance is increasing at every level in our educational and training system. The need for adequate counselling begins in the public schools and does not terminate until an individual finally retires from active participation in the labour force. The fact that career planning must begin in the public schools is apparent from the decision which will be required of the student as soon as he enters high school. Although it is true that students will be relatively free to move between the various streams of the Robarts Plan, substantial movement in this regard is hardly to be encouraged. The choice which must be made at the Grade VIII or Grade IX level is bound to be a critical one. Unless a tremendous effort is made to improve the state of our vocational guidance prior to this point unnecessary mistakes are bound to be made.

At this level, of course, it should not have to be emphasized that all student counselling should include consultations with parents and teachers as well. The need for comprehensive batteries of aptitude tests is also to be stressed. Perhaps more important than anything else, however, is the requirement that vocational counsellors have completely open minds as to the comparative advantages of the different alternatives open to the student. It is bound to take some time to instill our public school administrators and teachers with the idea that there is some advantage to a vocational education, as distinct from a straight academic program—even for brighter children. In the meantime the burden for developing such an awareness will fall upon the vocational counsellors. One point they should emphasize in this regard is the relatively dismal future confronting the straight academic drop-out as compared to his counterpart who has at least had some vocational preparation.

It should be obvious that we cannot afford to make vocational guidance a once-and-for-all proposition. Adequate facilities must also be made available at the high school and post high school levels. There is a particularly vital need at the point of transition between school and employment. All too often the student is left completely to his own resources once he leaves school. The schools no longer assume any responsibility for him and the National Employment Service has only begun to establish a youth counselling service. At this most critical juncture in their careers many youths are today without competent advice or counsel. Under these circumstances it is hardly surprising that so many of them cast about aimlessly for long periods of time.

Reflecting the view that many workers will have to undergo a considerable amount of retraining during their working lives, it follows that adult vocational guidance will also have to be much more fully developed in the future. The logical centre for such counselling is the National Employment Service. With this in mind it is our view that the Province should recommend to the appropriate officials in Ottawa that everything possible be done to strengthen the vocational guidance service within N.E.S.

Wherever vocational counselling is undertaken everyone who engages in it must be fully competent to carry out his responsibilities. Part time counsellors will no longer suffice. To qualify for career guidance, individuals should be fully conversant with available information on trends in the labour market, with the requirements called for in various trades and occupations, and with the latest techniques in aptitude testing. It goes without saying that they must also receive training in psychology in some depth. These matters are today so complex that no one can hope to begin to master them on anything less than a full-time basis.

In view of these considerations it is inconceivable to permit those who have not undergone specialized training to engage in vocational counselling. The work involved is too vital to be entrusted to partially trained amateurs. In the future, therefore, we would recommend that nothing less than university graduates with two years of additional specialized training in career guidance be employed for this purpose. We would also suggest that during the course of this training they be compelled to spend considerable time with the National Employment Service. Beyond this it is to be expected that anyone who makes a career of vocational guidance will make a determined effort to keep up with the latest developments applicable to his work.

Our recommendations with regard to vocational guidance are as follows:

(i) Vocational guidance must be accepted as a vital and integral part of our overall education and training system.

(ii) Expert counselling must begin in the grade schools and be continuously available to all students and workers until they finally retire from the labour force.

(iii) No effort should be spared to ensure that those who practice vocational guidance are fully competent to engage in such work.

(iv) Part-time vocational guidance in the schools should be eliminated as quickly as possible.

(v) In the long run it is our view that at least one full-time vocational guidance counsellor should be attached to every elementary and secondary school. The intensive nature of the job we must expect of vocational counsellors suggests that we must anticipate the need for a steady increase in the counsellor-student ratio. If we are not to do our students grave injustices, we must get away from once-a-year superficial appraisals and adopt much more intensive methods.

(vi) Wherever it is not practical to place a vocational guidance counsellor in every school (i.e. as in the case of small rural schools), competent teams of counsellors should be made available to circulate between the schools.

(vii) A vigorous effort must be made to increase the number and quality of vocational counsellors within the National Employment Service.

(viii) In addition to the need to make the pertinent material which has already been prepared more readily available to our vocational counsellors, a continuing effort must be made to ensure that they are kept as fully up to date as possible on the results of the research called for in the previous section.

ESTABLISHING COMMON STANDARDS AND FACILITATING UPWARD MOVEMENT WITHIN THE OCCUPATIONAL HIERARCHY

In this section of the Report we deal with two matters of growing concern. The first pertains to the need to develop common standards applicable to each of the various levels within the occupational hierarchy and the second relates to the desirability of facilitating upward movement between these various levels of skill attainment.

*The Need for Common Standards Applicable to the Various
Levels Within the Occupational Hierarchy*

One of the gravest needs in the field of manpower training and development is for common standards applicable to the different levels of skill attainment. Except for apprenticeship little or nothing has been done to develop common standards at any level on the vocational side of our educational and training system. This lack of common standards is particularly apparent at the secondary school level. Since most vocational students do not go on to Grade XIII, they are never subject to the same general set of examinations and employers have no common basis upon which to judge them. As a result students are often judged more on the basis of the particular school which they attended than on their performance. Because of this practice, mediocre students from schools with excellent reputations may find it easier to secure employment than better-than-average students from less renowned institutions.

The only way to overcome this problem is to gradually apply the Grade XIII principle of province-wide examinations to the terminal years of all vocational courses. In doing so every effort will have to be made to ensure that province-wide examinations are not applied in a manner which is likely to have a stultifying effect. There is a particular need to avoid the sort of levelling effect which can lead to a disproportionate emphasis on the least common denominator. Assuming that this can be avoided—and we believe that it can—we have everything to gain and nothing to lose from implementing such a change. In the meantime we can only rely on the "pressure of coercive comparison" to raise the standards of the poorer vocational schools relative to the better ones.

Beyond the high school level there is less reason for caution. Because of this, more emphasis can be given to what is fair to individuals —both as employees and employers—and to what is desirable from an economic point of view. To encourage employees to upgrade themselves, it is obvious that there must be some positive incentive. Aside from the increased remuneration which is likely to result therefrom, such incentive can best be provided by offering formal recognition for every significant advance in an individual's skill status. This in turn requires the establishment of various levels of competency to which are attached specific qualifications. These various degrees of proficiency and the standards which go with them should be made as universal as possible. Where this is not the case—as when programs are particular to specific firms—the general market value of the employee's newly acquired skills is normally reduced correspondingly. This is most unfair to the individuals involved and detracts from their motivation to upgrade themselves.

To the individual employer, on the other hand, such an approach may appear quite desirable. And yet, if every employer adopted a similar attitude the individual employer would lose as much as he would gain. Although it would be difficult for others to hire away his employees, it would be equally difficult for him to fill his needs by hiring from other firms. From the point of view of employers in general, therefore, this would seem to be a most shortsighted approach. We were very encouraged to find that the Ontario Division of the Canadian Manufacturers' Association agreed with us in this interpretation (Proceedings, p. 1521):

> Despite the aforesaid difficulties, there are undoubted advantages to be gained by having more uniform standards of trades qualifications in the manufacturing industry throughout the province or, if a uniform standard is not practical, providing a better means of identifying the level of skill and knowledge attained by a particular tradesman. Evidence of known standards of qualification would assist an employer or a prospective employer, to assess the competence of each tradesman; facilities for obtaining certificates of qualification would encourage tradesmen to improve and up-date their skills and, in the public interest, the workforce would become more flexible and more mobile.

Viewed from society's point of view, lack of common standards makes no sense at all. The efficiency of our economy depends upon the various types of labour flowing into those employments where it can be utilized most productively and thus earn the highest rate of return. Wherever possible we must strive to reduce those obstacles which prevent this from occurring. By facilitating movement between firms and industries, the adoption of common standards would serve to improve the effectiveness of the labour market. Thus, on grounds of efficiency, as well as on grounds of equity, everything possible must be done to develop common standards applicable to the various levels and types of occupational skills. The more universal these standards become, the greater their effectiveness is likely to be and the greater their potential contribution. In keeping with this spirit, we welcome the precedent which has been established under the apprenticeship program—where minimum nationwide standards have been adopted in a number of trades—and urge that the same practice be extended to as many other trades and occupations as possible.

To ensure that the standards established for the various levels in the occupational hierarchy are widely recognized, it is vital that an appropriate agency of the government be made responsible for specifying the desired standards and for supervising the certification—either voluntary or compulsory—of those with the requisite qualifications. In introducing such measures much can be learned from the work which has already been done by a number of private institutions. In the case of the Association of Professional Engineers of Ontario, for example, a great deal of progress has been made in establishing standards for various categories of technicians, for a special higher level classification of technologist, and for professional engineers. It stands to reason that all such groups in this Province must play a major advisory role in the promulgation of standards and in the establishment of certification procedures applicable to those they represent.

Although there must be close consultation on the part of the government with all such groups, we do not not believe that the Legislature should continue to delegate exclusive control in these areas to private groups. Instead it must itself assume ultimate control over these matters. This can be justified for a variety of reasons. In the first place, wherever certification is compulsory, the government has an obligation to see that the system is administered as fairly as possible. The government must make sure that those who wish to follow a particular career are not inequitably barred from so doing and must also protect the public from unduly high standards or from overly diligent policing of standards in order to restrict numbers. Even where certification is voluntary the government must be expected to play an expanding role. As particular standards are extended across inter-provincial boundaries and made more universal, for example, it is obvious that greater government participation will have to come with it.

Also to be stressed is the need to keep the standards for the various skills and occupations as flexible as possible. For reasons which have already been dealt with at some length in this Report, the standards called for at every level in our occupational hierarchy must be constantly adjusted to changing requirements. This will necessitate continuous contact and consultation among all those affected. At all costs, however, a strenuous effort must be made to prevent those having a vested interest in the preservation of particular standards from freezing them in order to serve some selfish and narrow purpose. This is another reason, of course, for insisting that ultimate control over these matters be vested in the government.

In establishing common standards at every significant level in the occupational hierarchy, and in facilitating the upward movement within this hierarchy which is called for in the next section of this Report, serious consideration should be given to the general principle which was advanced by the Ontario Division of the Canadian Manufacturers' Association (Proceedings, p. 1531):

> If we combine the continuing adult education concept with the specialization concept, and then add the concept of training by "blocks" of *common* knowledge and skill plus added "blocks" for specialization, one sees some hope for reducing an apparently complex and chaotic training problem to an understandable structure subject to prearranged systematic attack.
>
> By identifying common "blocks" of basic training and common "blocks" of production, office and field skills at progressively higher levels we *can*, if we will, provide a theoretical structure that will permit an individual to take training in an orderly way, moving *sideways* as often as necessary in response to changes in work requirements at the same level and moving vertically as far as individual ambition, capacity and effort, and opportunities provided by industry-government teamwork will permit.
>
> This process has no terminal point. As long as occupations can be analyzed as to requirements in knowledge and skill, theoretically at least, individuals can keep up with the times by readily adding new things to a firm foundation of things previously learned.

By devising appropriate tests or qualifications for attaining credit for each new advance in knowledge or skill, we could greatly extend the principle of common standards and provide for much more logical and ready movement from one level of proficiency to another.

*Facilitating Upward Movement Within
the Occupational Hierarchy*

Just as important as the promulgation of common standards at various levels in the occupational hierarchy is the need to provide for well defined channels of upward movement between these various levels. Although only a small fraction of our work force may avail themselves of the opportunity to move upward in the occupational hierarchy, it is essential that such movement be facilitated. As small as this fraction may be, it can be a critical factor in the efficient allocation of our total labour resources.

In keeping with this thinking we believe that there is one vital consideration which must not be overlooked in the development and maintenance of various common standards. This relates to the way in which individuals should be permitted to prepare to meet those standards. We do not believe that any standard should be so arbitrarily established as to provide for only one route to its attainment. We are particularly concerned about rigid academic requirements. Where a certain degree of academic proficiency is required it is usually specified in terms of a particular grade level, or the equivalent. We believe that where an individual is proficient in the particular academic skills which are likely to be necessary for him to meet the specified standard, any deficiencies he may have in other academic disciplines should be viewed leniently.

This is consistent with our general view that as few unnecessary obstacles as possible should be placed in the way of continuous movement up the occupational ladder for those who have the necessary drive and ability to so progress. Taking as an example a crude approximation of the occupational hierarchy on the craft and technical side of things (as portrayed by the accompanying chart), it is thus our firm conviction that everything possible should be done to facilitate movement from one level of proficiency to another. If this is to be the case we cannot afford a rigid adherence to general academic requirements. Instead we must be prepared to qualify them, at least in so far as that can be done without jeopardizing the individual's chances of completing the requirements at the next level of attainment. It likewise follows—and this is in line with some of our earlier recommendations with regard to apprenticeship—that intermediate levels of proficiency (halfway houses as it were) should be

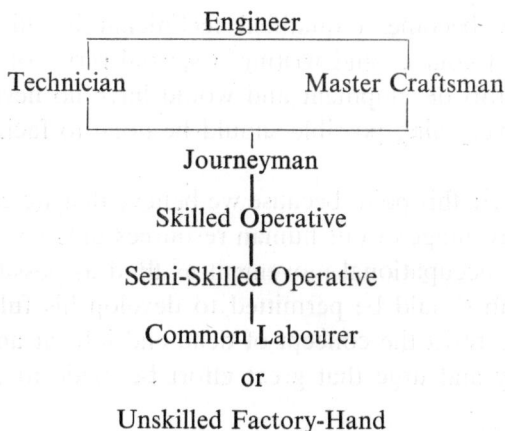

```
                      Engineer
              ┌──────────┴──────────┐
          Technician           Master Craftsman
              └──────────┬──────────┘
                     Journeyman
                         │
                  Skilled Operative
                         │
                Semi-Skilled Operative
                         │
                   Common Labourer
                         or
                 Unskilled Factory-Hand
```

established within each of the major categories in order to facilitate movement between the various levels of proficiency. In the words of the Social Planning Council of Metropolitan Toronto (Proceedings, pp. 1204-5):

> We would suggest that more graded courses be instituted wherever possible. There is a considerable difference between a course for a first class chef and short order cooks in an open kitchen. Just as there are several grades of stationary engineers, so there might be for many other occupations.
>
> This is particularly important for persons with limited ability and potential as well as those who have limited formal qualifications and yet have the potential to learn.

To illustrate our thinking more fully take the case of the common labourer in construction. Let us assume that he has been assigned to assist a group of tradesmen for a period of time and has picked up an interest in a particular trade. At the present time he cannot enter into apprenticeship in that trade unless he has the specified grade requirement or the equivalent. We believe that if he is willing to pick up those subjects which are absolutely essential to the trade in question, he should be permitted to enter into apprenticeship as soon as he has completed those subjects. Where graded certification is involved he might even be permitted to begin to work towards the minimum standard even prior to that time.

To further illustrate our thinking in this regard, consider the case of a journeyman. We are very encouraged by the fact that a journeyman can now become a qualified technician in this Province by attending night courses and writing a special series of examinations. We welcome this development and would have no hesitation in suggesting that everything possible should be done to facilitate this type of upgrading.

We emphasize this point because we believe that we can never hope to take full advantage of our human resources unless we learn how to make upward occupational movement as fluid as possible. We think that every man should be permitted to develop his full talents. For this reason we resist the concept of dead-end jobs at any level in our skill hierarchy and urge that great effort be made to eliminate such possibilities.

PROVIDING ADEQUATE NUMBERS OF VOCATIONAL TEACHERS

Just as vital as the provision of appropriate courses and the construction of suitable physical facilities is a sufficient supply of competent vocational teachers.[1] Without the latter, in fact, very little of lasting value can possibly be accomplished regardless of how satisfactory the courses or the physical facilities may be. Because the success of our vocational programs must ultimately depend so heavily on the quality of the teachers involved, it stands to reason that every effort must be made to ensure that an adequate supply is forthcoming.

To begin with, the training of vocational instructors must be placed on a par with the development of all other types of teachers at similar levels in our educational system. For reasons of status and prestige alone, we must develop equally high standards for vocational teachers as we have for their academic counterparts. Good vocational instructors must not only be able to teach the theory behind their subjects but must also be able to teach their practical application. In some fields this could readily lead to more taxing demands than those now served upon many academic instructors. In some instances it will no doubt mean that vocational teachers will have to embody a far more judicious combination of practical experience and theoretical knowledge than has ever been required of any other type of teacher.

---

[1]As important as the provision of vocational teachers is the development of capable personnel to administer vocational programs. Accordingly, what is said in this section with regard to the preparation of teachers is equally applicable to the training of administrators.

As well as adequate initial training, vocational teachers will have to be required to take periodic refresher courses in order to keep abreast of the latest developments in their fields. Although such a need is now discernible in many academic fields, it is not likely to become any more vital in these areas than in vocational subjects.

PLANNING—THE NEED FOR A PROVINCIAL ADVISORY COUNCIL ON VOCATIONAL AND INDUSTRIAL EDUCATION

It goes without saying that a manpower training and development program of the magnitude and complexity suggested in this Report cannot be developed or maintained without a great deal of planning. If such a program is to function effectively it must be based on an integrated and co-ordinated approach to education and training. Each facet of our overall manpower training and development program must be incorporated into a general plan which makes due allowance for all of our various needs in the field of education and training.

To appreciate the importance of planning in this field, a brief résumé of the responsibilities of vocational education planners will suffice:

—A continuing and careful watch must be kept on our current manpower needs and resources.

—Tied in with the former must be an on-going assessment of our future labour requirements.

—Our educational and training system must be geared to meet those requirements, with appropriate priorities being developed wherever financial limitations impose such a need.

—Preparing for the future will not only necessitate periodic overhauls of course content and of the physical plant and equipment required for education and training, but will also necessitate the provision of competent instructors in appropriate numbers and specialties.

—It will also require that consideration be given to the proper geographic dispersion of our educational and training facilities.

—Adequate attention must be devoted to the provision of vocational counsellors who are competent to guide students and workers.

—A great deal of thinking must go into the development and application of common standards at the different levels of our occupational hierarchy.

- —Just as much effort will have to be devoted to the structuring of the different levels of our educational and training system so that they readily flow into one another.
- —There will also have to be a continuing assessment of the respective responsibilities of all those concerned with education and training.
- —And finally, there will have to be a never ceasing effort to see whether we are taking full advantage of the varying interests, abilities and aptitudes of our population.

It should be obvious that none of these problems can be tackled on a haphazard or hit-or-miss basis. The stakes involved are too great to permit this to happen. Instead we are going to have to make a determined effort to plan our educational and training programs as far in advance as possible. We cannot afford to do less.

While the major responsibility for this planning must rest with the Provincial Department of Education and with local boards of education, we think something more is required as well. For this reason we are recommending that the Provincial Advisory Committee on Technical and Vocational Education (it might better be entitled the Provincial Advisory Council on Vocational and Industrial Education) be revitalized. The existing committee is not playing a useful role because it is not being properly utilized. Had it been serving the function we would anticipate for it, there might never have been the need for this Select Committee.

To our way of thinking this should be an independent public body composed of vocational educators, university experts and representatives from different private groups such as labour, industry, commerce and agriculture. It should meet at least quarterly, should serve as a forum for the discussion of current issues in vocational and industrial education, and should be free to issue public pronouncements where the need arises.

Although it should work very closely with the Provincial Department of Education, we do not believe that this Council should be part of the Department in any way, shape or form. To facilitate its efforts we would suggest that the Council be provided with sufficient funds to finance a small secretariat. We do not believe that it can properly play the role which we have in mind for it in the absence of such assistance. We likewise believe that where interested groups are asked to nominate candidates for this Council, they should be required to nominate persons who have an active interest in vocational and industrial education. The Council cannot possibly serve its intended purpose unless those appointed to it have sufficient interest in its activities to devote a good deal of time to it.

THE ADMINISTRATION OF VOCATIONAL AND INDUSTRIAL EDUCATION IN ONTARIO

It is this Committee's view that special emphasis will have to be given to vocational and industrial education in this Province for many years to come. There is a continuing need to prevent those who have never believed in anything but academic instruction from undermining the vocational side of our educational and training system. There is likewise a need—as we have emphasized previously—to ensure that our overall vocational and industrial education program is properly integrated and co-ordinated. In this connection it is essential that we so structure our high school and post high school programs that they readily flow into one another. This means that we must maintain a close link between our vocational courses in the high schools and general industrial education beyond that level.

To ensure that vocational and industrial education is not neglected in the future, this Committee recommends that a special division be created within the Provincial Department of Education. This division should be entitled the Division of Post Secondary School and Adult Education. It should be headed by a strong deputy minister[1] who has evidenced a firm appreciation for what can be accomplished through vocational and industrial education. For administrative and executive purposes he should be assisted by an equally strong and competent superintendent.

Although it might seem appealing to grant this new division complete control over all forms of vocational and industrial education which come under the jurisdiction of the Department of Education, this would not be practical. In particular it would not seem wise to split up the responsibility for secondary education along vocational-

[1]Immediately under the Minister in the Department of Education is the Chief Director of Education. Reporting to him are two Deputy Ministers; one who is responsible for the elementary schools and the other who is in charge of the secondary schools and a variety of other activities. We are proposing that a third Deputy Minister be added to the two now in existence.

academic lines. This would tend to divide responsibility for the secondary school program in a way which could have dire consequences. Aside from this exception, however, all other forms of vocational and industrial education under the jurisdiction of the Department of Education should be the responsibility of the new deputy minister.

As we would envisage the new division it could be organized as depicted in the accompanying chart. Should the apprenticeship program be made the entire responsibility of the Department of Education it would obviously come under the new division. For purposes of illustration the Director of Apprenticeship is thus included in the chart.

The other responsibilities which would logically come under the new division are indicated by the titles of the directors which are shown reporting to the new superintendant and deputy. These directors should be; a Director of Evening Classes at the Secondary School Level, a Director of Trade Schools and Technical Institutes, a Director of General Training in Industry (that is, all other forms of training besides apprenticeship), a Director of Training of the Unemployed, and a Director of Research, Counselling, and Curriculum Development. The latter is included to ensure that a special effort will be made to develop appropriate courses and teaching techniques for post-secondary school and adult education.

Although we recognize that this proposed new division cannot be expected to resolve all of the many administrative problems associated with vocational and industrial education in this Province, we are confident that it can be of great assistance in this regard. It will certainly facilitate greater integration and co-ordination of post-secondary school and adult education. If the new division works closely with those in charge of the full-time secondary school courses, it is also to be hoped that the same degree of integration and co-ordination between the secondary school programs and the post secondary school programs can also be realized. In the long run, of course, this is an absolute necessity.

There is one administrative problem which does not lend itself to any easy solution. This relates to the general position of vocational education in many of our school systems. Unless a great deal of care is taken to ensure that vocational educators receive the support and

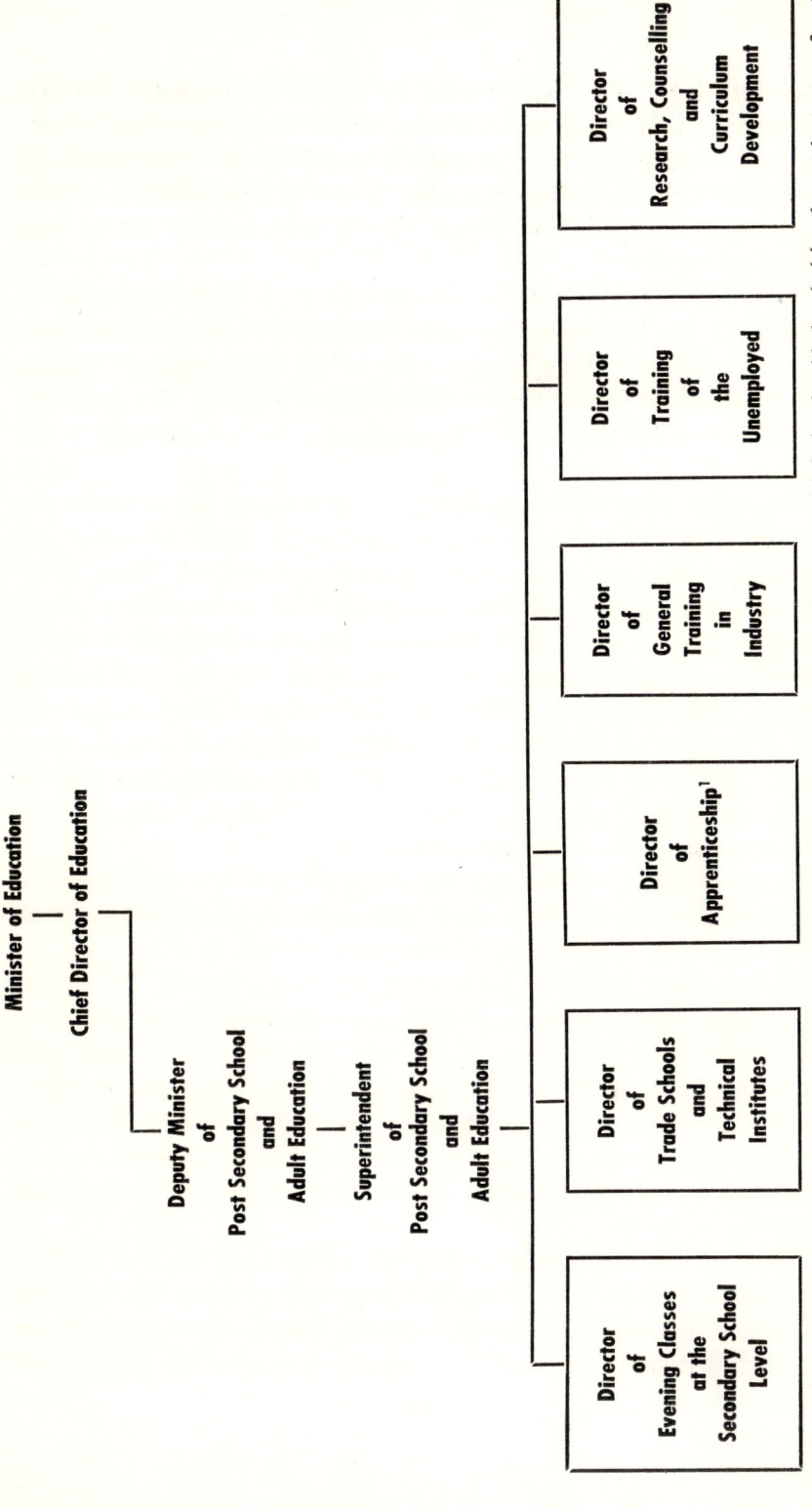

Minister of Education

Chief Director of Education

Deputy Minister of Post Secondary School and Adult Education

Superintendent of Post Secondary School and Adult Education

- Director of Evening Classes at the Secondary School Level
- Director of Trade Schools and Technical Institutes
- Director of Apprenticeship[1]
- Director of General Training in Industry
- Director of Training of the Unemployed
- Director of Research, Counselling and Curriculum Development

[1] The position of Director of Apprenticeship is shown in this chart in order to indicate where it would fit in should the decision be made to transfer the entire responsibility for apprenticeship to the Department of Education.

assistance which they deserve, their work is likely to be continually jeopardized by those who are prone to disparage any sort of vocational emphasis. Vocational education is particularly vulnerable to this sort of thing in composite schools. At least where the vocational schools are separate and distinct entities they have a fighting chance of proving themselves. In the composite school, on the other hand, vocational subjects are often treated as a form of second class education and may be given no chance to rise above that level. To reduce this possibility immense care is going to have to be taken to ensure that the right kind of men are made principals of the composite schools.

PART V

JUSTIFYING THE COSTS AND SHARING THE RESPONSIBILITIES FOR A COMPREHENSIVE EDUCATIONAL AND TRAINING SYSTEM

In this Part of the Report we seek to justify the increased costs of the comprehensive educational and training system which we have recommended and suggest a number of general guidelines designed to help determine how various groups in society can best share the responsibilities for such a system.

JUSTIFYING THE COSTS OF A COMPREHENSIVE EDUCATIONAL AND TRAINING SYSTEM

There is no doubt that the collective effect of implementing this Committee's many proposals will be to raise the outlays for education and training in this Province by a substantial amount. In view of the sizeable sums which are already being expended for this purpose it may seem presumptuous to call for even further outlays. Yet this is exactly what this Committee has chosen to do. There is no use minimizing the probable costs of our many recommendations at practically every level in our educational and training system.

We realize that a great deal has already been accomplished in Ontario and that a great deal is now being done. This will go a long way toward meeting the costs of the overall program which we have outlined. At the same time, however, much remains to be done. The fact that skilled immigrants are no longer turning to this country in sizeable proportions means that we must supply a higher and higher percentage of our needs in a number of critical fields. This will almost certainly require substantial increases in the size of our expenditures both at the trade school and technical institute levels and at the university level. A further illustration of the extent of the problem we face is provided by the inadequate state of our vocational guidance facilities. With occupations subject to such rapid change and with students and workers confronted with an ever-more bewildering complex of choices, there is no way of avoiding a tremendous increase in our career planning outlays. In this area alone it is reasonable to venture that we will soon have to double and even redouble our present level of expenditures. Increases of a similar magnitude will probably be required to continually upgrade the existing complement of vocational teachers and to prepare new ones. Substantial new outlays will also be required in a number of other areas.

The most effective way to justify these increased expenditures is to weigh the probable consequences of not undertaking them. It is our view that no nation or subdivision thereof can hope to survive as a prosperous economic entity unless the quality of its labour force keeps pace with developments in competing countries. Judging by what has been happening in Europe in recent years, nations in that part of the world are very much aware of the strategic importance of improving the skills of their labour force. Any nation which side-steps this challenge does so at its own peril. Unless we are prepared to support greater efforts in the field of education and training we are likely to find ourselves at a serious competitive disadvantage.

Closely related to the competitive position of the economy is the effect which education and training can have on our rate of economic growth. Economists now emphasize that an adequate level of expenditures on education and training is essential to a sustained rate of economic progress. This means that expenditures on education and training should be viewed as a form of capital investment which is just as capable of yielding a high rate of return as any other form of investment.

Speaking to this very point, Walter W. Heller, Chairman of President Kennedy's Council of Economic Advisers, made the following observation at a Policy Conference on Economic Growth and

Investment in Education sponsored by the Organization for Economic Co-operation and Development:

> Measuring the direct benefits of education in the form of increased productivity of the labour force—i.e., not allowing for either the consumption aspects or third party benefits of higher education—research on this frontier indicates that the rate of return on investment in college education in the United States is roughly comparable to the rate of return on business investment. Other studies show the rate of return for elementary and high school education combined as being substantially higher than that for college education. Thus, even using this type of measurement, private research to date suggests that the average rate of return on investment in formal education as a whole is higher than the rate of return for business investment. As just noted, this measurement understates the "payoff" on education since it assumes that all educational expenditures are investment expenditures with no consumption aspects and that all returns to education are direct, involving as it were, the transmission of existing knowledge rather than the extension of knowledge. Yet we know that some part of education is consumption and that the indirect—third party, or neighbourhood, or external, or extra-buyer—benefits of education, while difficult to measure (though obviously not difficult to coin phrases about), are significant.[1]

The fact that expenditures on education and training are a fruitful form of capital investment requires emphasis. Most people will accept the necessity of education and training as something which is vital to our individual welfare and general well-being. What is not always appreciated is the fact that the value of education and training can be measured in far more tangible terms as well. Failure to understand the full significance of this point has given rise to a tendency to visualize the costs of education and training in terms of expenditures on consumer goods, or as nothing more than administrative expenses, rather than as investment outlays essential to our economic growth and prosperity. When visualized from either of the former perspectives such costs may well seem prohibitive. When examined in the latter context, in contrast, they become vital forms of capital investment which can be expected to more than pay for themselves in the long run.

It is the responsibility of our leading citizens—especially in the fields of education and economics—to make the general public more

---
[1] Walter W. Heller, Chairman, Council of Economic Advisers, United States, Remarks before the O.E.C.D. Policy Conference on Economic Growth and Investment in Education. (Washington, D.C., October 16, 1961.)

aware of these considerations. Otherwise undue resistance to the increased outlays which education and training are bound to entail is unavoidable.

Although increased expenditures on education and training can be expected to contribute to a higher level of national income, this will not happen overnight. If there was no delay involved, then our national income would rise as fast as we expanded our outlays for education and training and we would not have to devote a larger share of our national income to these purposes. While this may be possible in the long run it is not possible in the short run. To help ensure a higher level of national income in the future, we must spend more of our national income on education and training now. In the words of the *Report of the Special Committee of the Senate on Manpower and Employment:*

> This situation must be viewed with a sense of urgency. Without any question we must devote a much larger proportion of our resources to education and training of all kinds—academic, professional, vocational, and technical.

Even in the long run, it should be admitted, we may not be able to count on the relatively painless opportunity of spending no more than the present proportion of our national income on education and training. As our manpower requirements shift steadily toward greater emphasis upon higher skills and more specialized knowledge, it follows that we will probably have to devote proportionately greater time and effort to education and training. Unless and until this trend is reversed, we will have to be prepared to allocate a higher proportion of our national income to this end. It is our view that such an increase would be well worth the expenditure. This reflects our belief that among society's assets there is none more precious than that which is inherent in our human resources. In the words of our Governor-General:

> Now as perhaps never before, Canada's future progress, prosperity and security are dependent on the educational level, the technical knowledge and the skills of our people.[1]

There is at least one other point which should be made with regard to the increased costs which are bound to flow from our many propo-

---

[1] Proclamation of His Excellency, Governor-General G. P. Vanier, D.S.O., M.C. declaring the week of May 29 to June 4, 1961 as "Commonwealth Technical Training Week in Canada", February, 1961.

sals. This relates to the cost of those programs which are designed to increase the employability of the employable unemployed. Whether we are providing marketable skills to drop-outs, to inmates of our penal institutions, to the disabled, or to those who are just plain unemployed, there is one major consideration which should be kept in mind. In the long run it would probably cost society far more to maintain employable unemployed on some form of social security or charity than it would to enhance their employability to the extent that they can at least lead reasonably productive and self-sufficient lives. An example cited by the Social Planning Council of Metropolitan Toronto (Proceedings, p. 1213) will suffice to illustrate this point:

> The Civil Rehabilitation Branch of the Federal Department of Labour estimated that the care of a group of over 5200 handicapped men and women with a total of almost 4000 dependents was costing their family or their community some $3,878,000 a year. 80% of these handicapped persons were without any earnings at all and half of them were receiving public assistance. After rehabilitation, the same 5200 people together earned some $9,633,000 annually. They were self-supporting members of society, leading useful lives and making worthwhile contributions to the community.

Experience such as this reveals how shortsighted it would be—again looking at it strictly from an economic point of view—to reject retraining programs for employable unemployed solely on the grounds that it might cost too much.

In taking the position which we have in this section of the Report, we do not believe that economic considerations alone (such as the relationship between education and training and economic growth) are the only important ones. Modern society is becoming increasingly complex. Without adequate education and training it is obvious that our students and workers will be confronted with increasingly dismal prospects. To avoid undue frustration in this regard we feel that society has an obligation to the individual to ensure that he has every possible opportunity to thoroughly prepare himself for the realities of the future world of work.

Although this is not a matter which is central to our general terms of reference we think we would be derelict in our duties if we did not express some further thought with regard to the matter of opportunity. Equality of opportunity has always been a central tenet of those who espouse the cause of the free enterprise system. As education and training become increasingly essential to the successful man of the future, it stands to reason that equality of opportunity will have little or no meaning at all unless it is interpreted to encompass equality of access to all forms of education and training. For all practical purposes we now have such equality up to and including the final year of high school. Although there are many forms of assistance available to needy students beyond this level, there remains much to be done for those who seek access to higher education and do not have the wherewithal to finance themselves. While we welcome the efforts which have already been made at the post-high school level, we urge that consideration be given to providing even more assistance to those who have the necessary qualifications to benefit from higher education.

SHARING THE RESPONSIBILITIES FOR A COMPREHENSIVE EDUCATIONAL AND TRAINING SYSTEM

Turning to the matter of the respective responsibilities of different groups for the provision of adequate educational and training facilities, it becomes very difficult to be as definite as we would like to be. One thing is certain, however: unless all those involved—the different levels of government and various private bodies such as labour, industry, commerce and agriculture—are willing to approach this matter in a co-operative spirit, much harm will be done to our overall manpower training and development program. This co-operation must not only include general support for a comprehensive education and training system but must also include a willingness to forego whatever traditional dogmas may apply to particular interest groups in this area. In the words of the Ontario Federation of Labour (Proceedings, p. 556):

> Until both companies and unions agree that the general interest transcends the individual prerogative, we shall get nowhere either in economic expansion or in the efficient training and use of manpower.

Education and training have become so essential in the modern world that every level of government, every organized group and every individual must support our collective efforts in these areas as unselfishly and fully as possible.

Responsibility for providing a basic education necessarily rests with the government. At the very least we must look to public authorities to provide us with sound elementary and secondary school education. Beyond this we feel that it can also be agreed that the state has a responsibility to provide for a range of other facilities. Among these we would number trade schools, technical institutions and special facilities for training various categories of adult workers. The extent of the government's responsibilities in these areas must ultimately depend on the amount which is accomplished by private groups and institutions. The more training that is carried on by industry itself, for example, the less the pressure on public facilities. The same is also true of charitable organizations in the field of rehabilitation of disabled and handicapped persons.

In all those areas of education and training where the primary responsibility inevitably lies with society at large, it is incumbent on private groups and individuals to lend the state their full support. On the part of industry and commerce, for example, it may at times have to embrace the lending of equipment and personnel to schools on a temporary basis. On the part of virtually all groups it will almost certainly have to include active participation in advisory groups designated to keep our vocational education programs as up-to-date as possible. The work of the Ontario Industrial Education Council has been especially valuable in this respect. We would encourage an expansion of its work and would recommend that the government subsidize its activities to the extent that this may be necessary. We would also suggest that an attempt should be made to widen the representation presently found within local chapters of the O.I.E.C.

In those areas where the state bears the greatest share of the responsibilities, the costs have become so great that no one level of government is capable of financing all of them. As it now stands the bulk of the responsibility has fallen on local municipalities. Except for trade schools and technical institutes, most of the heavy expenditures (for elementary and secondary school education) are made at the local level. Because our municipalities and townships have not had sufficient financial resources to support these activities, they have had to be provided with more and more assistance from the provincial and federal governments. We would expect this trend to continue and would suggest that the only possible alternative is a complete takeover by the Provincial Government. Although there would be a number of advantages to such a takeover (especially with regard to the matter of equalizing educational opportunities across the Province), we believe that the associated disadvantages would more than outweigh the advantages. By permitting flexibility at the local level, municipal autonomy has stimulated a competitive atmosphere which by and large has been very healthy. It has led, however, to a marked disparity in the quality of education in different parts of the Province. Greater consolidation among small urban and rural areas, instead of more centralized control at the Provincial level, would seem to be the most effective way of overcoming this deficiency. At least for the present we would recommend no more drastic action.

Beyond the high school level the situation becomes more debatable. Although we have suggested a greater role for the government at these levels, this should not be taken to mean that we are satisfied with the role which industry and commerce are presently playing. Far from it. It is our view that industry should be providing more on-the-job training either in the form of apprenticeship or its facsimile. We agree with the observation of the present Director of the Vocational Training Branch of the Federal Department of Labour, when he said:

> Industry in Canada has not assumed the degree of responsibility for providing training for its workers that European industry has.[1]

Large industry in particular must do much more than it has been accustomed to in the recent past. Far more serious than the performance of larger enterprises, however, is the status of training in many small and medium size firms. Except for informal on-the-job training, provision for manpower development is often non-existant in these enterprises. In many cases they are not large enough or do not have sufficient equipment to support any kind of formal training. Where this is the case there should be a pooling of the efforts of several firms—either in the same industry or in different industries—to promote a co-operative training scheme. Where lack of interest or the ready ability to pirate skilled help away from other firms is the problem, there is probably nothing which can be done. Here the only

---

[1]C. R. Ford, A paper presented to the Canadian Conference on Education, Cited in *Education and Employment*, Education Centre Library, The Board of Education for the City of Toronto (August, 1962), p. 95.

hope may lie in a gradual tightening up of the labour market for skilled personnel.

Although we would be reluctant to suggest that general subsidies be paid to industry to encourage more on-the-job training, there are certain types of assistance which should be offered. Where a firm does not have access to first-rate evening courses, either at the high school or post-high school level, direct subsidies to facilitate the importation of competent instructors or for travel to other communities should be extended. Similarly, where an isolated firm is willing to do more training but lacks certain vital pieces of equipment, consideration should be given to special grants for that purpose. In keeping with some of our earlier recommendations we would also suggest that generous assistance be granted to firms which are willing to engage in intensive training measures in order to equip their existing work force to hold onto their jobs in the face of expected changes in skill requirements. In so far as the operation of formal apprenticeship schemes is concerned we have also suggested that some sort of financial inducement be provided.

Organized labour must also bear some share of the responsibility for the present state of our training system. In the building trades, for example, the willingness of unions to take into their ranks and vouch for the skill of workers who have not undergone any form of formal apprenticeship training is one of the reasons why the apprenticeship program has been so deficient. In industrial undertakings, on the other hand, undue emphasis on seniority may have at times led to greater managerial resistance to retraining programs than might otherwise have been the case. Even where seniority is not rigidly adhered to for purposes of selecting candidates for retraining or upgrading, more emphasis will probably have to be given to ability to learn as opposed to ability to do.

Although we have been candid in our comments about labour and management efforts in the field of education and training, we do not wish to minimize some of the outstanding achievements which numerous institutions among both groups have to their credit. During our investigations we have been made aware of some excellent training programs operated by individual firms and industries. Both in the way of apprenticeship and in less formal fashions there are many firms in this Province which have accomplished a great deal. Similarly, on the union side, there have been some encouraging signs. Some of the craft unions, for example, have sponsored special courses to provide their members with the most up-to-date developments in their trades. In addition a number of industrial unions have developed and promoted excellent apprenticeship programs for the maintenance trades in their industries.

It is not our purpose to disparage or detract from these efforts in any way. What we do feel is that they have been confined to too few unions and companies and that they have often been far too limited in their scope. What we are suggesting is that far more of this sort of thing must be done if unions and employers are to contribute as fully to our overall educational and training effort as they are obviously capable of doing. While the bulk of the responsibility in this regard invariably falls on management we do not feel that the role of either group is to be minimized. It is our belief that on-the-job training is most effective when both labour and management pool their efforts and earnestly work together. They will fail themselves and society at large if they do not learn to do so on a more extensive basis than has been the case in the past.

Not to be overlooked in this discussion is the responsibility of the individual. Aside from the obligation to support the development and maintenance of a comprehensive educational and training system, it is up to every citizen to take as full advantage of the education and training which is made available to him as he can usefully absorb. While this Committee does not subscribe to compulsion in the latter regard (except with respect to the specification of a minimum age for school-leaving purposes), we do believe that every effort should be made to acquaint as many people as possible with the extent of the range of courses available. Where necessary adequate incentives should be offered in order to make retraining and upgrading as attractive as possible. For those who refuse to take advantage of the available training facilities and who consequently remain a serious charge on the public purse there is no easy answer. Instead of compelling them to take training—where that is the only hope they have for ever finding employment—we would suggest that the public assistance they receive be kept relatively unattractive. If this does not induce them to better themselves they are likely to be the type of misfits which no one can salvage.

SUMMARY AND CONCLUSIONS

IN bringing this report to an end, we would like to reiterate briefly the general objectives which we have come to believe must underlie Ontario's future efforts in the field of vocational education and training and repeat our many specific proposals in summary form.

GENERAL OBJECTIVES

(1) The "holding power" of our schools must be increased as much as possible by having them offer a sufficient variety of courses to appeal to the differing interests, abilities and aptitudes of our student population.

(2) Especially during the early years of our vocational education and training system, more emphasis will have to be placed on ability to adapt as opposed simply to the acquisition of a limited range of manipulative skills.

(3) Much more will have to be done at the post-secondary school level to provide students with sufficient specialized knowledge to make them readily employable.

(4) As an extension of the previous point there is the need to think more of education and training as a continuing process in which the securing of employment no longer marks the terminal point in a worker's vocational preparation but merely denotes a change in method, orientation and emphasis in this regard.

(5) In keeping with the spirit of the previous objectives, provision must be made to meet the upgrading and retraining needs of special groups of individuals by means of programs designed for each of the following purposes:

(i) Salvaging drop-outs and enhancing their employability;
(ii) Training unemployed workers who have obsolete skills or who are relatively unskilled.

(iii) Upgrading of employed persons who otherwise would be displaced from their jobs;

(iv) Facilitating the integration of immigrants into constructive employment;

(v) Rehabilitating inmates of our penal institutions;

(vi) Rehabilitating disabled and handicapped persons.

(6) To take full advantage of the comprehensive educational and training system outlined above, we must place much more emphasis on manpower research—especially with regard to occupational forecasting — and we must establish competent vocational counselling services.

(7) To ensure efficient utilization of our human resources, everything possible will have to be done to provide every student with as much education and training as he is capable of effectively absorbing.

(8) Finally, and perhaps most important of all, there is the need to think in terms of a much more co-ordinated approach to education and training.

SPECIFIC RECOMMENDATIONS[1]

The Robarts Plan

(i) There must be a stepped-up and continuing effort to build up the status and prestige of the non-academic streams in the new multi-stream system.

(ii) A greater effort must be made to make the general public more conversant with the purposes and advantages of the multi-stream system.

(iii) Special efforts will have to be made in sparsely settled regions of the Province in order to realize the full advantages of the multi-stream approach. These efforts should include consideration of further consolidation of school districts in small urban and rural areas. Additional grants may also have to be considered to assist local boards of education in these localities.

(iv) Agricultural options must be strengthened in rural areas of the province. At the same time, however, ample provision must be

---

[1]Not all of our many specific recommendations are included in this summary presentation. A number of relatively minor proposals, which are subsidiary to those listed here, have been left out.

made for training in other vocational subjects for rural youths who do not intend to seek permanent employment in agriculture.

(v) A continuing effort must be made to establish and maintain a proper balance between the practical and the academic content of the various vocational courses.

(vi) A greater effort must be made to develop vocational options which are appropriate to the present and foreseeable employment patterns in the localities in which they are offered.

(vii) In the long run there should be less emphasis on specialized vocational training at the high school level and more emphasis on broadly-based vocational training designed to make students as adaptable as possible.

(viii) In the future, more and more of our attention on the vocational side of education will have to be focused on the Business and Commerce stream.

Trade Schools

(i) The trade schools should continue and strengthen the work which they have been doing in connection with apprenticeship programs in the Province.

(ii) They should make their facilities available and offer courses in as many other areas as possible. They should be prepared to initiate and extend courses in non-apprenticeable trades and occupations, to offer pre-apprenticeship training, to provide assistance to employers seeking to upgrade the skills of their workers, and to meet any other related training needs which may arise.

(iii) In the future we must expect the trade schools to do more in the way of providing vocational school graduates with the specialized skills which may be required of them for immediate employment.

(iv) Over the years we must be prepared to build many more trade schools and to disperse them more widely across the Province.

(v) In keeping with the broader orientation of the trade schools, consideration should be given to the possibility of a new name for these schools.

Technical Institutes

(i) The technical institutes should be encouraged to expand both their full-time and part-time programs as rapidly as possible.

(ii) Although major reliance for the training of technicians will have to be placed on full-time day courses, day-or-block-release and sandwich courses must also be introduced.

(iii) Over the years we must be prepared to build more technical institutes and to disperse them more widely across the Province.

(iv) Consideration should be given to curtailing further expansion of our engineering schools, at least at the undergraduate level, until we realize a better balance between our needs at the university level and those at the technical institute levels.

(v) While the Ryerson Institute of Technology should be permitted to become a senior institute of technology in the Province, we question whether it should be permitted to aspire to anything beyond that level.

The University Crisis

To provide for the greatly expanded university enrolment which is to be expected in this Province in the next decade, much more aid must be made available to the universities as soon as possible.

Apprenticeship in the Building Trades

(i) Due and proper recognition must be afforded workers who successfully complete an apprenticeship program in the building trades.

(ii) To this end, compulsory certification should be applied to all trades which can be expected to benefit from it. To avoid abuse of such a scheme, compulsory certification should not be applied to any trade unless it is accompanied by legislation or regulations consistent with the following recommendations.

(iii) Where compulsory certification is put into effect in any trade, provision must be made for classifications denoting appropriate journeymen-level specialties and/or varying grades of proficiency within the trade. Only where such designations prove to be absolutely unnecessary or completely unworkable should they not be made mandatory.

(iv) Where graded certification is introduced in any trade, training for the junior levels of certification should take the form of a modified version of the journeymen apprenticeship program.

(v) When introducing compulsory certification in any trade those now in the trade should be given four or five years to establish their competency and bring their proficiency up to the necessary level.

(vi) Having implemented a compulsory certification scheme the government would then have some obligation to see that an adequate number were flowing into the various trades. To begin with much more should be done to make students and the general public more aware of the advantages of apprenticeship and of the pros and cons of a career in one of the building trades.

(vii) More pre-apprenticeship training for drop-outs and unemployed workers should be made available.

(viii) The age limit for apprenticeship should be abolished.

(ix) Provision must be made to ensure that vocational high-school students, who wish to enter an apprenticeship program, receive adequate credit for any progress which they have made while in school. An appropriate series of tests—both practical and theoretical—should be devised for this purpose.

(x) Such tests should be open to anyone who has acquired some knowledge and experience in a trade and wishes to enter an apprenticeship program in that trade.

(xi) No firm should be allowed to bid on any government construction project unless it normally employs an appropriate complement of apprentices.

(xii) Administration of the apprenticeship program in the building trades must be improved.

(a) If it is decided that the best way to bring this about would be to turn over the entire responsibility for the apprenticeship program to one or other of the two departments presently involved—

the Department of Labour and the Department of Education—then there is only one logical choice. It would have to be turned over to the Department of Education. If this is the ultimate decision the Director and the present staff of the Apprenticeship Branch would have to be transferred to the Department of Education. There would have to be a compatible shift in the administrative set-up of the latter in order to make this practical.

(b) If instead, it is decided to maintain the present division of responsibilities, a strenuous effort will have to be made to improve the relationship between the Apprenticeship Branch in the Department of Labour and the staff of the trade schools.

(c) Regardless of how it is decided to expedite the administration of the apprenticeship program in the building trades in this Province, the decision must be made soon and, once made, must be given full support by all concerned.

(xiii) Where possible, apprentices should be indentured to local joint apprenticeship committees or to the appropriate branch of the government rather than to individual employers.

(xiv) There must be more inspection of the on-the-job side of apprenticeship in order to ensure that proper training is being provided.

(xv) Consideration should be given to the development of multi-trade apprenticeship programs wherever these seem to be required.

(xvi) The apprenticeship program should be administered in as flexible a fashion as possible.

(xvii) There should be a separate Provincial Advisory Committee for each one of the apprenticeable trades. These committees should be strictly advisory in nature and their membership should be subject to more turnover than in the past.

(xviii) Local joint apprenticeship committees should be established to supervise the operation of the apprenticeship program at the local level.

(xix) Care must be taken to see that the apprenticeship program is administered so as not to discriminate against any workers—union or non-union.

(xx) The use of the terms "designated" and "non-designated" trades should be discontinued. In the future, there should only be one basic distinction. The certified trades would be those for which a certificate would be required to practice the trade and the non-certified trades would be those for which there was no such requirement.

(xxi) Consideration should be given to the possibility of expanding apprenticeship in the building trades to trades which are not now covered.

Apprenticeship in Other Trades and Occupations Outside of General Industry

(i) In the main, the same set of recommendations as have been suggested in the case of the building trades should be extended to apprenticeship in other trades and occupations outside of general industry. This would apply particularly to the use of apprenticeship in the training of such occupations as the motor vehicle trades, barbering, hairdressing, cooks, and the printing trades, to name only a few.

(ii) In some of these trades (i.e. barbering and hairdressing) provision should be made for complete training in schools as well as under an apprenticeship program.

Apprenticeship in General Industry — The Need for a Separate and Distinct Approach

(i) Minimum standards applicable to various types of apprenticeship in general industry should be drawn up and provision should be made for a Provincial seal of approval to be affixed to those company certificates which are awarded under programs which meet those standards.

(ii) Where feasible, special standards appropriate to the apprenticeable trades in particular industries should be worked out on an industry-wide basis.

(iii) Multi-trade apprenticeship standards appropriate to the skill-mix requirements of different types of industrial maintenance work should also be worked out wherever practical.

(iv) Where firms are not large enough to maintain their own apprenticeship programs, they should be encouraged to join in co-operative undertakings with other employers.

(v) Consideration should be given to some form of modest financial reimbursement to those firms which operate apprenticeship programs in compliance with the minimum standards laid down at the Provincial level.

(vi) All firms in general industry should be compelled to register their apprenticeship programs with the appropriate authorities.

(vii) To assist in implementing the above proposals, there should be established a Provincial Advisory Committee for Apprenticeship in General Industry, composed of a cross section of labour and management representatives in the field of manufacturing.

(viii) As sufficient local interest develops, similar committees should be established at that level.

Other Forms of Training in General Industry

(i) Industry must be encouraged to carry a greater share of specialized pre-employment training than it has in the past.

(ii) In the hope that its own self interest will eventually dictate an appropriate course of action in this regard, it is urged that industry continually re-assess its position in this matter.

Special Programs for Training or Retraining
Particular Categories of Adult Workers

(i) At the local level, full-time co-ordinators of adult education should be employed wherever it is economically feasible to do so.

(ii) Special adult education centres should likewise be established wherever it is possible to do so.

Salvaging Drop-outs and Enhancing Their Employability
>(See also, Training Unemployed Workers Who Have Obsolete Skills or Who Are Relatively Unskilled)

(i) The policy of the Provincial Institute of Trades whereby no drop-out is accepted into a Program 5 (Training of the Unemployed) course until at least six months after he leaves school should be continued and be applied across the Province.

(ii) Youth camps which combine both work experience and further education and training should be operated for unemployed juveniles and young adults, especially during times of unduly heavy unemployment.

Training Unemployed Workers Who have Obsolete Skills or Who are Relatively Unskilled

(i) Unemployed workers should not be compelled to undergo training or retraining.

(ii) Instead, greater financial assistance, relative to the payment due to an unemployed worker under the Unemployment Insurance System, should be made available to unemployed workers who are willing to undergo training.

(iii) While undergoing training, either the unemployed worker's equity in the Unemployment Insurance Fund should be protected or he should receive a higher training allowance than those who are not eligible for or those who have exhausted their unemployment benefits.

(iv) Those who are involved in the training of unemployed workers must become more familiar with and make due allowance for the non-financial problems of the unemployed worker.

(v) Continued and extensive use must be made of the course entitled "Basic Training for Skilled Development" in the training of unemployed workers.

(vi) Increasing emphasis must be placed on the development of special techniques for the teaching of adult workers.

(vii) For the time being at least, it should be left up to local municipalities to initiate training and retraining courses for unemployed workers.

Upgrading of Employed Persons Who Otherwise Would be Displaced from Their Jobs

(i) Every encouragement must be given to individual firms to upgrade their workers for more demanding jobs, especially where displacement is the only alternative for such workers.

(ii) Financial assistance for this purpose should be made available to employers under Program 4 (Training in Co-operation with Industry) of the Technical and Vocational Agreement.

(iii) Program 4 should be interpreted in as broad and flexible a fashion as Program 5 so that basic training for skill development can be included as part of any upgrading program.

Facilitating the Integration of Immigrants Into Constructive Employment

(i) Where lack of fluency in the English language is a problem, emphasis should be placed upon the use of condensed courses which concentrate on the fundamentals of the language and which stress the acquisition of practical work-oriented English.

(ii) Where sufficient numbers are involved, immigrants who lack fluency in the English language should be taught trade and related subjects by bilingual instructors.

(iii) Bilingual instruction should be used most sparingly, however, in the teaching of English.

(iv) Wherever examinations and tests in subjects other than English are involved, immigrants who lack fluency in English should either be permitted to answer questions in their native language, or be permitted the use of an interpreter.

(v) Where immigrants are concerned, particular care must be taken to ensure that grade or equivalency qualifications for specific trades and occupations are not enforced unfairly.

(vi) Where sufficient numbers apply for Program 5 Courses, the courses should be so structured and sub-divided as to meet the specific needs of particular categories of immigrants.

(vii) Besides Program 5 courses, part-time, evening, and extension courses should also be made available to immigrants. Consideration should also be given to the establishment of special full-time programs designed to better prepare the immigrant for work immediately upon his arrival in Canada.

Rehabilitating Inmates of Penal Institutions

(i) The rehabilitation work which is being undertaken in our penal institutions should be continued and strengthened.

(ii) The Department of Reform Institutions should work as closely as possible with the Department of Education in this area.

Rehabilitating Disabled and Handicapped Persons

(i) Every effort should be made to reduce our institutionalized and dependent population by providing them with some degree of employability.

(ii) Primary consideration should be given to the subsidization of the work of private groups who are already active in this field.

(iii) Where necessary, the entire responsibility for these matters should be transferred to the public domain.

(iv) More sheltered workshops and sheltered hostels must be established as soon as possible. Where private groups are not prepared to operate such facilities, even with government assistance, the government should move into this field on its own initiative.

The Role of Private Trade Schools and Correspondence Schools

(i) Private trade schools and correspondence schools as a group should not be prohibited or regulated out of existence.

(ii) Only where a particular trade or occupation appears to be especially susceptible to infiltration by illegitimate private schools should consideration be given to exclusive public sponsorship of the training in question.

(iii) In all other cases there must be constant vigilance and repeated inspections by comptent persons familiar with the training in question to ensure that schools are offering nothing less than they purport to offer.

Supervisory Training and Management Development

(i) Industry must be encouraged to sponsor more programs to develop competent personnel at all levels in management.

(ii) In this area, the government should concentrate its efforts on the development of a general education system which is capable of turning out high-quality students who can readily respond to these types of programs.

(iii) The government should also encourage a strengthening of the Business and Commerce stream of the high school vocational program and promote more advanced work in the managerial sciences at the technical institute and university levels.

(iv) The government should only sponsor special programs of its own where no other alternatives are available.

(v) All government programs in this area should be administered and co-ordinated by the Provincial Department of Education.

Research—A Neglected but Vital Need

Much more emphasis must be placed on manpower research than has ever been the case in the past.

Forecasting Changes in the Nature and Composition of the Labour Force

(i) Primary attention must be given to the development of as much information as possible on the current and future needs of the economy for trained manpower.

(ii) At least two types of occupational forecasts must be developed; one for the immediate future and one for the more distant outlook.

(iii) In both cases, criteria must be developed for use in deciding the reliability of the results which are forthcoming.

(iv) In both cases, as well, it will be necessary to develop sound assumptions as to the future development of the economy upon which to base the occupational forecasts.

(v) In the case of the more immediate forecast, much use can be made of the material which is available to the National Employment Service. To provide for further information from this source, it is recommended that the National Employment Service should make use of the power it now possesses to require all employers to list their vacancies with it on a monthly basis.

(vi) Consideration should also be given to the use of properly constructed surveys designed to determine the needs which employers anticipate in the future.

(vii) Every effort must be made to see that all of the information developed on this subject is made available to those who need it most as quickly as possible.

Development and Improving our Educational and Training Methods

(i) Material must be developed on what is likely to happen to the skill content of particular jobs as well as information on the number of such jobs which are likely to be available in the future.

(ii) Much more effort must be made to explore how the various skills called for in different occupations can best be imparted.

(iii) Related to this is the need to greatly improve teaching and training techniques at all levels in our vocational education and training system.

Assessing the Record

(i) There must be continuing audit of our educational and training system in relation to the demands made upon it.

(ii) Among other things this should include an ongoing evaluation of the role of the labour market as an allocator of manpower.

Responsibility for Research

(i) Responsibility for research in all of these areas should be shared jointly by the federal and provincial governments.

(ii) For this purpose, close liaison should be maintained between those at the two levels of government who are responsible for this work.

(iii) Within the Provincial Government, responsibility for forecasting our future manpower needs should be shared jointly by the Departments of Labour, Education, and Economics and Development.

(iv) For this purpose, a special committee of those most concerned with the need for this type of information should be established at the operating level to oversee and co-ordinate its development.

(v) Responsibility for the other types of research called for above must rest largely with the Department of Education.

(vi) This Department must become far more research-oriented than it has ever been in the past.

(vii) Much more staff and financial resources must be provided for manpower research in the future.

(viii) Until a competent staff can be brought together at the government level, and probably even after that, ample use should be made of the research talents of outside experts.

Vocational Guidance

(i) Vocational guidance must be accepted as a vital and integral part of our overall educational and training system.

(ii) Expert counselling must begin in the grade schools and must be continuously available to all students and workers until they finally retire from the labour force.

(iii) No effort should be spared to ensure that those who practice vocational guidance are fully competent to engage in such work.

(iv) Part-time vocational guidance in the schools should be eliminated as quickly as possible.

(v) In the long run it is our view that at least one full-time vocational guidance counsellor should be attached to every elementary and secondary school.

(vi) Wherever this is not feasible (i.e. as in the case of small rural schools), competent teams of vocational guidance counsellors should be made available to circulate between the schools.

(vii) A vigorous effort must be made to increase the number and quality of vocational counsellors within the National Employment Service.

(viii) In addition to the need to make the pertinent material which has already been prepared more readily available to our vocational counsellors, a continuing effort must be made to ensure that they are kept as fully up to date as possible on the results of the research called for in the previous section.

Establishing Common Standards and Facilitating Upward Movement Within the Occupational Hierarchy

(i) Common standards should be developed at as many levels in our occupational hierarchy as possible.

(ii) A determined effort should be made to facilitate upward movement within the occupational hierarchy.

The Need for Common Standards Applicable to the Various Levels Within the Occupational Hierarchy

(i) Province-wide examinations should be introduced at the end of the terminal years of all vocational courses at the secondary school level.

(ii) Beyond the secondary school level, as at that level, every significant advance in an individual's skill status should be subject to official recognition.

(iii) This recognition should be made as universal as possible.

(iv) For this and other reasons, an appropriate agency of the government must bear the responsibility for establishing the standards which should apply at various levels in the occupational hierarchy.

(v) This agency must also bear the responsibility for establishing the certification procedures—voluntary or compulsory—under which individuals may seek official recognition for the degree of proficiency which they have earned in terms of the above standards.

(vi) In establishing common standards and appropriate certification procedures at different levels in the occupational hierarchy, this agency should work in close consultation with affected parties.

(vii) At all costs, however, a strenuous effort must be made to prevent those having a vested interest in the preservation of particular standards from freezing them in order to serve some selfish and narrow purpose.

Facilitating Upward Movement Within the Occupational Hierarchy

(i) Wherever practical, alternative routes should be kept open for the attainment of the standards applicable to the various levels in the occupational hierarchy.

(ii) In addition a vigorous effort should be made to so design the prerequisites and standards at the different levels in the occupational hierarchy to permit advancement from one level to another without undue difficulty.

(iii) This means that a rigid adherence to general academic requirements must be avoided except where they are absolutely essential to enable progress from one level of proficiency to another.

(iv) An effort should also be made to establish intermediary levels of proficiency (halfway houses as it were) between the various major levels of proficiency.

Providing Adequate Numbers of Vocational Teachers

(i) Every effort must be made to ensure that an adequate and competent supply of vocational teachers is forthcoming.

(ii) The training of vocational teachers must be placed on a par with the development of all other types of teachers at similar levels in our educational system.

(iii) As well as adequate initial training, vocational teachers will have to be required to take periodic refresher courses in order to keep abreast of the latest developments in their fields.

*Planning—The Need for a Provincial Advisory Council
on Vocational and Industrial Education*

(i) A great deal of planning will be required to develop and maintain a manpower training and development program of the magnitude and complexity suggested in this Report.

(ii) The final responsibility for this planning (except perhaps in the case of apprenticeship) rests with the Provincial Department of Education and with local boards of education.

(iii) The Provincial Advisory Committee on Technical and Vocational Education (it might better be entitled the Provincial Advisory Council on Vocational and Industrial Education) should be revitalized to offer assistance in this planning.

(iv) This Council should be provided with sufficient funds to finance a small secretariat.

(v) Where interested groups are asked to nominate candidates for this Council, they should be required to nominate persons who have an active interest in vocational and industrial education.

(vi) This Council should be independent of the Department of Education, should serve as a forum for the discussion of current issues in vocational and industrial education, and should be free to issue public pronouncement where the need arises.

*Administration of Vocational and Industrial
Education in Ontario*

(i) Special emphasis will have to be given to vocational and industrial education in this Province for many years to come.

(ii) For this reason, a Division of Post-Secondary School and Adult Education should be established within the Department of Education.

(iii) It should be headed by a strong deputy minister who has evidenced a firm appreciation for what can be accomplished through vocational and industrial education.

(iv) For administrative and executive purposes the new deputy minister should be assisted by an equally strong and competent superintendent.

(v) Aside from the full-time vocational high school courses, the new division should embrace all other forms of vocational and industrial education which come under the jurisdiction of the Department of Education.

(vi) Every effort will have to be made to ensure that those who are in charge of the full-time vocational courses at the secondary school level work closely with those in charge of the new division.

(vii) In order to ensure that vocational educators receive as much support and assistance as their academic counterparts, immense care is going to have to be taken to see that the right kind of men are made principals of the composite schools.

Justifying the Cost of a Comprehensive Educational and Training System

(i) Every effort must be made to inform the public of the vital role which vocational education and training can play in keeping our economy competitive and in ensuring a satisfactory rate of economic progress.

(ii) Attention should be focused on the fact that education and training represent one of the most fruitful forms of capital investment which can be undertaken.

(iii) Consideration must be given to the provision of more assistance to those who have the necessary qualifications to benefit from higher education but do not have the financial means to afford it.

Sharing the Responsibilities for a Comprehensive Educational and Training System

(i) Every level of government, every organized group and every individual must be encouraged to lend their full support to our collective efforts in the field of vocational education and training.

(ii) Local municipalities must continue to bear the responsibility for the provision of sound elementary and secondary school education.

(iii) The senior levels of government will have to lend increasing financial assistance to local authorities to enable them to properly carry out this responsibility.

(iv) The government must also bear the ultimate responsibility for the provision of a range of other facilities, including trade schools, technical institutes and special facilities for training various categories of adult workers.

(v) Where possible, however, private institutions should be encouraged to carry a greater share of the burden in these areas.

(vi) In those areas where the government bears the responsibility for providing adequate educational and training facilities, it is incumbent on private groups and individuals to lend their full support.

(vii) Both employers and organized labour should be expected to greatly expand their activities in the area of education and training.

(viii) Where necessary, public assistance should be made available to labour and management groups which are willing to become more active in the field of manpower training and development.

(ix) Aside from the obligation to support the development and maintenance of a comprehensive educational and training system, it is up to every citizen to take as full advantage of the education and training which is made available to him as he can usefully absorb.

APPENDIX

SUBMISSIONS WERE MADE TO THE COMMITTEE BY THE FOLLOWING:

Professor Harold A. Logan

The International Correspondence Schools (Canadian), Limited

International Brotherhood of Electrical Workers

Ontario Council of the Hotel & Restaurant Employees & Bartenders' International Union, AFL-CIO-CLC

Ontario Federation of Labour, CLC

Ontario Industrial Education Council

Brantford Board of Education

Mr. Ken Hawkins, Rehabilitation Branch, Department of Health

Mr. John Plewes

Mr. George A. Cummings

Mr. A. Klarman, Registrar of Trade Schools, Department of Education

Mr. Rowland G. Hill, International Union of Operating Engineers

Mr. Thomas Davis

Mr. H. M. Boreski, General Secretary of the Fort William-Port Arthur & District Labour Council

Iron Workers District Council of Eastern Canada

Ontario General Contractors Association and the Toronto Construction Association

The Ontario Provincial Association of the United Association of Journeymen and Apprentices of the Plumbing and Pipefitting Industry of the United States and Canada

Canadian Union of Operating Engineers

Mr. A. N. Deslauriers

Federal Department of Indian Affairs

Social Planning Council of Metropolitan Toronto

Collegiate Institute Board of Ottawa

Tool and Die Manufacturers' Association

Anglican Church Army

Provincial Council, United Brotherhood of Carpenters & Joiners of America

Italian Immigrant Promotion Centre, (COSTI)

Ontario Provincial Association of Journeymen, Barbers, Hairdressers, Cosmotologists and Proprietors, International Union of America

United Automobile Workers of America

Canadian Restaurant Association

Association of Professional Engineers

Council of Printing Industries of Ontario

Ontario Beauty Schools Association

Electrical Contractors Association

Association of Canadian Hungarian Technicians, Technical Tradesmen, Inventors and Technical Improvers

Volkswagen Canada Limited

Drouillard Barber School Limited

The Ontario Barber School and Instructors Association

The Institute of Chartered Engineers of Ontario

Procor Limited, Oakville, Ontario

The London Chamber of Commerce

The Ontario Welfare Council

The Ontario Vocational Education Association

The Volunteer Education Program for Unemployed Persons (Toronto)

The Society of Plastics Engineers

The Canadian Association for Adult Education

Canadian Manufacturers' Association, Ontario Division.